CREATING SMALL HABITATS FOR WILDLIFE IN YOUR GARDEN

First published 2000 by
Guild of Master Craftsman Publications Ltd,
166 High Street, Lewes, East Sussex, BN7 1XU

ISBN 1 86108 188 X
A catalogue record of this book is available from the British Library

Photographs by:
Niall Benvie: pp 56–7
Dave Bevan: pp iv, 43, 50, 89
Josie Briggs: all photos on p 4, Hawthorn on p 27, Hawthorn on p 40, p 78,
oxeye daisies on p 92, p 115, garden rockery p 122, pp 158, 166
Mark Hamblin: pp 84–5
Julian Slatcher: pp iii, 6–7, 24–5, 112–13
GMC Publications/Ed Gabriel: pp 65, 130–1, 148–9
Brian Lowry: all other photographs

Cover photographs by:
Julian Slatcher: background image
Steve Young: Great spotted woodpecker
Dave Bevan: all other photos

Illustrations by Josie Briggs

Cover and book design by Fran Rawlinson
Typefaces: Felt Tip and New Baskerville
Colour origination by Viscan Graphics (Singapore)
Printed and bound by Kyodo Printing (Singapore) under the supervision of
MRM Graphics, Winslow, Buckinghamshire, UK

CREATING SMALL
HABITATS FOR WILDLIFE
IN YOUR GARDEN

Josie Briggs

GUILD OF MASTER CRAFTSMAN PUBLICATIONS

Contents

A quiet revolution

Most gardeners enjoy butterflies, like this peacock, visiting their gardens

One of the smallest woods in Britain – 3m² (10ft²) – occupies a corner of my back garden. It consists of a single silver birch with an understorey of seedling oaks, carpeted with periwinkle, ivy, primroses and spring bulbs. My garden also contains a mixed native hedgerow, wildflower meadow, cornfield, rocky hillside, informal pool and marsh area. All of these, plus the creatures they attract, coexist happily with the human inhabitants; there are also seating areas, lawn, a goldfish pond and vegetable patch, as well as a shed, garage and drive. You may be thinking that I own a large garden, smallholding or even a country estate, but my garden is a typical small plot, no larger than most suburban gardens.

There are fashions in gardening, longer term than those on the catwalk but just as real. As the countryside has become more regimented, gardens have become less formal. Rectangular lawns, rows of bedding plants and clipped privet are giving way to irregular curves and cottage-garden-style borders. Concerned about pollution and rural habitat loss, more gardeners are using organic methods of cultivation, eschewing chemicals and actively encouraging wildflowers and creatures to colonize their gardens.

This trend has been noticeable in recent television series on garden design. Offered a professional design and landscaping of their gardens before the cameras, many candidates ask to incorporate wildflower meadows, wildlife ponds or overgrown areas where their children can play. Newsagents' shelves are stocked with magazines containing items on nature and garden wildlife.

Campaigns against the relentless march of 'progress', which drenches fields with chemicals and replaces woods and wetlands with concrete, often make local and national news. Many farmers and local councils are beginning to change their management of the countryside, making their land more wildlife friendly. Hedges and tree belts are being planted alongside roads and fields. Careful timing of cutting roadside verges allows wildflowers to flourish. Recent concerns about the decline of some of our once common songbirds, however, show there is still a long way to go.

We can all play our part in wildlife conservation. A million acres of land are safe from developers and factory farmers. These acres are the private gardens, backyards, allotments and smallholdings in the towns and country. This huge area, which is increasing annually, has the potential for becoming a nationwide network of nature reserves.

1

2

3

4

5

6

Only a few years ago, most gardens were as ecologically barren as the surrounding farmland. Now a quiet revolution is in progress. A reduction in the use of pesticides, herbicides and artificial fertilizers is making our gardens safer and friendlier to wildlife.

It is not only the owners of larger gardens who are joining this revolution. Tiny plots can hold a variety of habitats. In his excellent book, *Making a Wildlife Garden,* pioneering wildlife gardener, Chris Baines, tells of a friend who manages a sand dune, chalk grassland, acid bog and hay meadow, each in a concrete tub on a terrace of a few metres (yards) square. Even window boxes and pots on balconies can play their part when planted with nectar-rich flowers to sustain passing insects.

Of course, the whole garden does not have to become a wilderness. Small habitats can be included in the design, with the rest of the plot cultivated more conventionally. Be warned though; wildlife gardening is addictive and you may find yourself, like me, introducing more and more habitats. This is not a problem – properly managed, such a garden can be very attractive and interesting.

My dictionary defines a revolution as a 'fundamental complete change'. Managing a garden to make it wildlife friendly may require a change in direction from 'traditional' methods. The result is a sense of peace and wellbeing in a garden that is really alive. The rewards are immeasurable.

CLOCKWISE FROM TOP LEFT
1   Formal pool, with goldfish, about one year after it was made
2   Cornfield annuals in front of the mixed native hedgerow
3   Dry stone wall and gravel area
4   Colourful spring containers
5   Informal wildlife pool soon after it was made
6   Spring meadow in its first year

NATURE'S BALANCE

Working with ecology

A certain amount of courage is needed to attract
wildlife into a garden; neighbours may misunderstand
your uncut lawn and wildflowers in the borders.
However, a wildlife-friendly garden need not be an
unkempt wilderness. If correctly managed, it will be at
least as attractive as its manicured neighbours.

But why should we want to invite wildlife into our
gardens at all? In many respects, gardening often seems
to involve battling against nature to keep away weeds
and pests. There are excellent reasons, however, for
attracting wildlife into your garden.

RURAL HABITAT LOSS

Since intensive farming began in the 1940s, Britain has lost:

- 95% of its wildflower meadows;
- 72% of its lowland heaths;
- 50% of its remaining woodland;

- 50% of its lowland marshes;
- tens of thousands of miles of hedgerows;
- most country ponds.

One important reason is to counteract habitat loss in the countryside. In Britain, over 1.7 million acres of rural landscape – an area larger than Greater London, Berkshire, Hertfordshire and Oxfordshire put together – have been lost to development over the last half of the twentieth century, and most of this during the last 20 years. The Countryside Movement – formed in November 1995 to protect the British countryside and to campaign and educate about rural issues, and now amalgamated with the Countryside

Heath grassland is an endangered habitat

Most country wetlands have been drained for agriculture or building land

Alliance – estimates that an area five times that of Watford is urbanized each year. These figures are alarming. Although new hedges and tree belts are being planted in some regions, and roadside verges are being managed more sympathetically, it will be a long while, if ever, before such large-scale damage can be put right.

More and more gardeners, concerned about damage to their countryside, are turning to organic methods, rejecting the use of chemicals and encouraging wildlife on to their land.

HUMAN BENEFITS

Managing a wildlife-friendly garden is more than just a selfless ideal: people benefit too. Lower levels of garden chemicals result in a healthier environment for everyone, with less pollution of food crops, soil and ground water. Such a garden can be exciting, absorbing and educational, bringing interesting events and visitors throughout the seasons. As many native plants rival their domesticated relatives in beauty, wildlife areas can also be extremely attractive.

Recently, scientists have found some disturbing connections between agro- and garden chemicals, and health problems in humans.

CHEMICALS, POLLUTION AND HEALTH

Organic gardening is good for people as well as wildlife. Some of the recent health and pollution scares associated with the use of chemicals in gardening and agriculture are as follows:

In 1994, domestic water supplies in many areas of Britain were found to contain pesticide levels above the European Community (now called the European Union) Directive maximum.

A study in the USA showed that children whose parents use garden pesticides and herbicides have four times the risk of contracting cancer of connective tissue.

Male fruit farm workers exposed to high levels of pesticides take twice as long, on average, to become fathers.

Lawn mowers powered by petrol emit exhaust fumes with up to 50 times the levels of harmful pollutants as those produced by car engines: catalytic converters are recommended.

In parts of the USA, fertilizers used on lawns and golf courses cause serious contamination of ground water.

In 1995, many British lettuces were found to be contaminated with residues from unauthorized pesticides, including vindozolin, which causes birth defects in rats.

Again in 1995, some carrots contained up to 25 times the permitted levels of organophosphates (used against carrot fly). Organophosphates can cause stomach cramp, nausea and other health problems.

Traces of organochlorine insecticides and fungicides, including DDT, have been found in tree bark in some very remote areas of the world.

CHILDREN AND WILDLIFE GARDENS

Cast your mind back to your childhood. Which was the best place to play: the park with its closely mown grass and carpet bedding, or the waste ground with scrub, tall grasses and all sorts of interesting rubbish dumped among the vegetation?

Children and wildlife gardens are made for each other. Youngsters can let their imaginations run wild in gardens where the grass is allowed to grow and there are wild areas to explore (providing, of course, that wildlife like poisonous spiders and snakes do not make their home in the area).

Wildlife gardens are educational, and can foster a knowledge of and concern for the environment and ecology. In my role as home tutor, I sometimes take children out into their own gardens and encourage them to look at the plants and dependent creatures in a new way, and they enjoy these lessons the best. Encourage your children to help design, create and manage your garden habitats to help them learn to respect and enjoy nature.

There are some dangers if you have young children, but they are the same as in any garden. Open water, even in a small pond, is best avoided until children are old enough to understand the danger. Some plants have poisonous fruits, the worst being woody nightshade and yew. With very small children, it is best to avoid plants with attractive, brightly coloured berries unless you know they are safe. Nettle patches and thorny shrubs are other things to avoid until the children are older.

UNDERSTANDING ECOLOGY

Wildlife gardening is a branch of organic gardening. Stated simply, organic cultivation involves co-operating with nature, not fighting against it. To be successful at making and maintaining garden habitats, especially in a small space, it is necessary to have some understanding of the relatively young science of ecology – the study of how living things relate to each other and their surroundings.

This began in earnest around the turn of the twentieth century when Ernst Haeckel, a German biologist, suggested that it should be a separate field of biology. He coined the term from the Greek 'oikos', meaning home or place to live, and 'logos', meaning science.

Nectar from this orchid is sipped by small herbivores like burnet moths

Most scientists believe that life has evolved over thousands of millions of years, continually adapting to and colonizing the slowly changing world. As a result, communities of living organisms developed, learning to depend on one another for their mutual benefit. As well as relating to and reacting with each other, living things also interact with the elements of the non-living world – sunlight, air, water, rocks and soil – referred to collectively as the environment.

As life spread over the world's surface, plants and animals adapted to form woodland and forest communities, either evergreen or deciduous depending on climate or position. Some colonized aquatic habitats: rivers, lakes and oceans. Others spread to marshy ground, rocky hillsides, mountain meadows and arid grasslands.

There are set roles for the inhabitants to play in all of these ecosystems (or habitats); they work together to form food chains and food webs, recycling materials and ensuring that a balance amongst species is maintained.

FOOD CHAINS AND WEBS

The first link in any food chain is provided by green plants. Unlike animals, plants can take carbon dioxide and water (inorganic substances) and turn them into complex, energy-rich foods, using the power of sunlight. Plants are eaten by herbivores which, in turn, are eaten by carnivores. Larger carnivores may then eat the smaller ones.

The final link in the chain is the least glamorous, though just as essential as the rest. When animals and plants die, their remains must be decomposed and the substances of which they are made returned to the environment for recycling.

Bloodworms, which live in pond mud, are midge larvae. Both larvae and adults are important members of food chains

A FOOD WEB OF A FRESHWATER POND

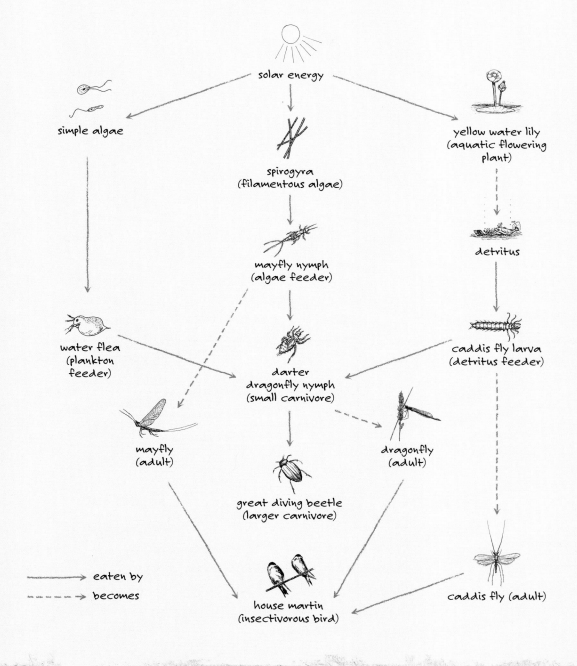

simple algae

solar energy

spirogyra
(filamentous algae)

yellow water lily
(aquatic flowering
plant)

mayfly nymph
(algae feeder)

detritus

water flea
(plankton
feeder)

darter
dragonfly nymph
(small carnivore)

caddis fly larva
(detritus feeder)

mayfly
(adult)

dragonfly
(adult)

great diving beetle
(larger carnivore)

eaten by

becomes

house martin
(insectivorous bird)

caddis fly (adult)

Animal excreta must also be processed. The life forms that carry out this task are mainly hidden away and unnoticed: bacteria, fungi and scavenging invertebrates work silently in soil and compost, dead leaves, rotting wood and the detritus on pond bottoms.

In practice, food chains are rarely this simple. Many living things move between different ecosystems as they grow and mature. A vegetarian or scavenger in one habitat may grow up to become a predator in another. In addition, many animals move between habitats during the day and night, and with the seasons. All this leads to food chains interacting to form complex food webs.

An example of a food web for a freshwater pond is given on page 13. This shows the transfer of energy from the sun, via aquatic algae and other plants, through herbivores and finally to carnivores. If one component of this web were removed it would adversely affect the whole system, with members further down the web going short of food.

It is interesting to note that this food web is not confined to the water. Aquatic larvae become airborne insects and provide food for birds. Tadpoles become frogs which leave the pool to hunt down slugs and snails on the land. Clearly, habitats are not isolated systems, but interact with one another. Damage to one will affect all in some way.

In a well-balanced community, every variety of living thing has its own place and its own task. The balance between plants, herbivores, carnivores and decomposers prevents the numbers of any one species from becoming too large. Species live together in agreement, avoiding competition with their cohabitants wherever possible. Only overcrowding or an external disruption will upset this balance.

ECOLOGY IN THE GARDEN

One of the main reasons that cultivated gardens have problems with pests and diseases is that, generally, they are not managed in the way nature intended. Of course, gardeners are perfectly happy for plants, or at least the permitted varieties, to grow in their gardens, but they are not so keen to welcome the next link in the food chain – the small vegetarians that feed on their prize specimens. Aphids, caterpillars and slugs are actively discouraged, often being killed with toxic chemicals. Yet these creatures are essential in well-balanced communities, including gardens. Destroy them, and the predators at the next step of the food chain will starve. Ladybirds, dragonflies and many birds cannot eat plants directly, but depend on so-called garden 'pests' for their food.

Spraying the greenfly on roses, for example, can actually make matters worse in the long term. Their predators – ladybirds, hoverflies and lacewings – if they survive the spray, must then go elsewhere in search of food, or starve. When the next group of aphids flies in the following day, there will be no insects to prey on them and control their numbers, which means spraying yet again. This will happen even if 'safe' insecticides, which kill the pests and leave the predators alive, are used.

It does take courage to do nothing when aphids infest your roses and lupins, reproducing rapidly and decorating the foliage with glistening honeydew. Soon, however, the larvae of ladybirds and hoverflies will appear, munching their way through hundreds of aphids, and in a surprisingly short time the plants will be practically clear of their attackers.

THE IMPORTANCE OF BIODIVERSITY

Scientists have found that habitats containing a greater variety of species are healthier, more stable, and recover more quickly after damage than those with a limited number of species. For example, an 11-year study by scientists from the universities of Minnesota and Montreal showed that natural, species-rich grassland recovered far more quickly after severe drought than did cultivated areas with fewer plant varieties.

Mimicking nature by introducing as many different plants as possible into the limited space of our gardens really does reduce pest and disease problems.

Another problem with many modern gardens is that only a limited selection of plants are allowed to grow in them: grass, fruit and vegetables, herbs, ornamental annuals, biennials and perennials, and approved shrubs and trees. Nature's way, on the other hand, is to colonize an area with as many plant species as possible. Ancient, virgin countryside is incredibly rich in the number of different plants that grow and intermingle there.

Many wildflowers, such as this foxglove, are as beautiful as any cultivated flower

Organic gardeners should try to imitate this, making use of companion planting and creating borders with shrubs, flowers, herbs and vegetables all jostling together. This is a healthy way of gardening: pests and diseases have difficulty finding their host plants amongst all the others, and cannot spread easily even if they do, while pollinating and predatory insects are attracted in large numbers by mixed planting.

Many pests and diseases are specific to certain plants or groups of plants, for example, lupin aphids will attack only lupins. In a monoculture, pests and diseases spread easily, but if different plants are mixed together, it is more difficult for pests and diseases to jump from one plant to others of the same type. Pests which find their host plants by smell or colour have difficulty finding their hosts among the jumble of a mixed border.

WEEDS OR WILDFLOWERS

To attract insects, birds and other creatures it is important to grow some native flowers, shrubs or trees because natural food chains and ecosystems have developed based on these plants. Many herbivorous insects are able to feed on very few plant varieties. Caterpillars of the orange-tip butterfly, for example, only feed on four varieties, including garlic mustard and lady's smock, which are generally treated as weeds by gardeners.

Plants introduced from abroad, on the other hand, generally have far fewer dependent insects than the native flora. There is no reason not to grow attractive aliens in your garden, and many do have wildlife value (discussed in Chapter 7), but do include a selection of native species among them.

See tables in Chapters 2–6

With the present trend towards wildlife gardening and conservation, more gardeners are growing native plants in their gardens, and plant and seed companies are meeting this demand by making more varieties available. You need to be discerning, though, because some native plants are prolific seeders and will take over your garden in no time. Others have deep, spreading root systems or creep over the ground and quickly smother a flowerbed.

This still leaves a huge choice of wildflowers suitable for growing in gardens. As your confidence grows, you will probably wish to introduce more varieties, including less 'showy' plants that nevertheless are important for wildlife or are themselves endangered in

NATIVE OR NATURALIZED

It is not easy to define 'native plant'. Many botanists call plants that were present when rising sea levels cut off Britain from the rest of Europe, about 5500BC, native to Britain. During the following centuries mankind brought many other species, by accident or design, from other lands and many of these have escaped and established their own places in the countryside. This is still happening today.

Many garden escapees have become naturalized, and it is impossible to classify some plants as wild or garden. In the mild climate of Cornwall, for example, montbretia (crocosmia), normally considered a garden plant, has colonized large regions of cliffs. In other parts of Britain the butterfly bush (*Buddleia davidii*), originally brought from China by plant hunters, has escaped and spread. Although there are some problems with over-vigorous escapees, most have found their niches and become important members of local communities.

In the tables of wildflowers I have given, I have not stuck to natives in the strictest sense, but have included species with wildlife value that arrived later and have become naturalized.

Wildflowers attract many creatures. This peacock butterfly is taking nectar from burdock flowers

in their natural habitat in the countryside. Examples of wildflowers suitable for small gardens are given in the following chapters, according to habitat type.

HIDING PLACES

We can provide for herbivores by growing suitable food plants, but it is important that we also provide for their predators. These creatures need shelter in which to hide or hibernate. This could take the form of ground cover, dry stone walls or log piles; it can also be provided by leaving the pruning of woody and herbaceous plants until spring.

Keeping gardens neat and tidy actually discourages predators from sheltering in them. Ground beetles, which consume slugs and snails, lurk under stones or in dense, undisturbed ground cover during the day, while clusters of ladybirds hibernate over winter in twiggy shrubs and climbers like honeysuckle and field maple.

See Table 1.1 Page 23

If you dare to relax a little, more beneficial creatures will set up home in your garden, where they will work to keep 'pest' numbers down. Leave a pile of woody prunings or leaf litter undisturbed and hidden behind a shrub; this will provide shelter for beetles, hedgehogs and other small and useful creatures. Managing part of your grass as a flower meadow, leaving it uncut for much of the year, encourages spiders and frogs to hide there, in the damp vegetation.

Ground beetles prey on slugs, vine weevil grubs and other small creatures

DEATH AND DECAY

The recycling of dead organic matter and animal excreta, returning the elements of life back to the environment ready for use by the next generation, is vital in nature and in gardens. Recycling is carried out by members of the final link of food chains, the decomposers and scavengers. Gardeners should encourage their activity by providing suitable living conditions for them.

One way to do this is through sympathetic soil cultivation. Soil is not simply an inert medium for plants to grow in but is, in itself, a complex habitat for communities of living things. Many of these, including bacteria, fungi and worms, feed on dead organic matter and, in so doing, improve soil texture and release nutrients in a form that plants can use. Fertile soil contains up to a billion bacteria per gram. The activity of bacteria, and other soil-dwelling decomposers, can be encouraged by adding organic matter (manure,

Spiders are useful 'pests', being predators of flying insects

Ladybirds, larvae and adults, feast on aphids and other small herbivores

compost or leaf mould) to soil as a mulch, or by digging it into the top layer. Never use garden chemicals, including synthetic fertilizers, as these can destroy much of the soil's microscopic life forms and lead to long-term problems.

The annual loss of leaves from deciduous trees results in leaf mould, due to the work of fungi and small scavengers on the fallen leaves. Leaf litter itself is a rich wildlife habitat, containing thousands of microscopic life forms as well as larger ones, such as woodlice and beetle grubs. These creatures feed on decaying leaves, breaking them down into humus and plant nutrients.

Dead wood is vital in woodlands. Fungi and woodboring insects gradually soften it and return its nutrients to the soil. Decaying wood prunings are very useful in an organic garden. Because they are slow

These Armillaria mushrooms, related to the parasitic honey fungus, are harmless. They grow on tree stumps and dead wood

The bracket fungus on this dead log is helping to decay the wood

Grass flowers are rarely seen in well-tended gardens today

to rot, shredded bark and twigs make an excellent long-term garden mulch. Larger twigs and branches can be piled in a corner where they will be used as shelter and food by decomposers and other small animals.

Every organic garden should include a compost heap or bin, where the natural bacterial decay of dead vegetation is speeded up. Fungi and invertebrate scavengers, like woodlice and worms, may also be active in a compost heap. Add grass mowings, uncooked kitchen vegetable waste, most weeds and garden waste (but not the seed heads of weeds or the roots of perennial weeds), shredded newspaper and old cotton clothes. This also takes some of the burden off our rapidly filling landfill sites.

GARDEN HABITATS

While we are looking at ways of attracting wildlife, I should mention the most valuable of all: the provision of habitats in which wildlife can really feel at home. Briefly, such habitats could include small native trees, shrubs and climbers, a rockery or dry stone wall, a log pile, leaf litter, a pond, bog or marsh area, and a wildflower meadow. These do not have to be large; small versions can fit into most gardens, backyards, patio gardens and even window boxes.

Because living things move between habitats, as we saw earlier, it is good to include several different habitat types in your garden if possible. This also increases biodiversity, resulting in a healthier garden that needs less attention. One reason for this is that different plants need different nutrients; if only one or a few varieties grow in a patch, the soil quickly becomes deficient in some nutrients, hence weakening the plants. Also, with just a few varieties, plant-specific pests and diseases can build up quickly. (See The importance of biodiversity, page 15.)

ATTRACTING WILDLIFE INTO YOUR GARDEN

- Use organic cultivation methods:
  - avoid using pesticides, fungicides and herbicides: these disrupt food chains, may pollute soil and plants, and may be toxic to humans
  - use organic, slow-release fertilizers, such as blood, fish and bone or seaweed meal, instead of artificial ones; this leads to healthier plant growth
  - make your own compost and leaf mould to recycle organic matter
  - incorporate plenty of organic matter into the soil to increase soil life and improve soil texture and fertility
  - grow several plant varieties together to reduce the spread of pests and diseases attract natural predators to control 'pests'

- Grow some native trees, shrubs, climbers and wildflowers: these support more wildlife species than do imported or hybridized plant varieties

- Don't be too tidy; leave uncut grass, ground-cover plants, fallen leaves and log piles to shelter small predators and their prey

- Provide a number of different habitats to attract a wide range of wildlife and allow it to flourish

TABLE 1.1

ATTRACTING NATURAL PREDATORS OF GARDEN 'PESTS'

Predator	Prey	Attract by	Remarks
Birds	Aphids, caterpillars, grubs, slugs, snails	Bird table, bird bath, bird boxes, pond, trees and shrubs, feed in winter	
Centipedes	Insects, slugs	Ground-cover plants, leaf litter and log piles for shelter during day	Light brown; longer legs than millipedes
Frogs and toads	Slugs, woodlice, small insects	Pond, ground-cover plants or long grass for shelter	

Frog

Predator	Prey	Attract by	Remarks
Ground beetles	Cutworms, eelworms, leatherjackets, slugs, insect eggs	Ground-cover plants, leaf litter and log piles for shelter during day	Black beetles
Hedgehogs	Slugs, cutworms, millipedes, wireworms, woodlice	Log or leaf piles by hedge or among shrubs	
Hoverflies	Aphids	Yellow, flat or open flowers, eg pot marigold, yarrow	Larvae eat aphids; adults eat nectar

Hedgehog

Predator	Prey	Attract by	Remarks
Lacewings	Aphids	Mixed flowers	Larvae eat aphids
Ladybirds	Aphids and other small insects	Mixed flowers	Larvae and adults eat aphids
Spiders	Flying insects	Log piles, dry stone walls, long grass, dense planting	Some spin webs, others hunt

DOWN IN
THE WILD WOOD

Woodland habitats

At first sight it seems challenging to mimic the
mighty forest in a small garden. It is certainly possible,
however, to include a woodland habitat as part of a
garden through the selection of suitable trees,
shrubs and woody climbers.

WOODLAND HISTORY

A woodland in spring is a light, airy place with a variety of wildflowers beneath the trees

Britain's natural state is to be covered with trees. When the last Ice age ended, around 10,000 years ago, virgin forest sprang up to replace the ice sheets. As a result, most of the native plants and animals, including ourselves, evolved and developed to live in woods or woodland clearings.

Only the constant activities of mankind keep our land from reverting to forest. Left unattended, wasteland, meadow, marsh, heath and gardens would become woodland again in a few decades. First, colonizing birch and ash would take hold, followed by stalwarts like oak and beech.

Long before the wholesale destruction of ancient woodland that occurred during the twentieth century, mankind had an influence on the landscape. Our medieval ancestors harvested much of the forest as a renewable source of timber. Their periodic cutting back of hazel, willow, hornbeam and lime understorey trees provided wood for furniture, ships and fuel. The thin wands that sprouted from coppiced trunks were woven into baskets and wicker fencing. Towering above this shrub layer, standard oaks, ash, beech and Scots pine were allowed to grow tall and straight until their timber was needed for buildings or ships. When a standard was felled, the temporary clearing quickly filled with colourful wildflowers as bright sunlight touched the ground for the first time in decades. Eventually, tree saplings grew to fill the space again.

The woods managed in this way became the richest in species. The constantly renewed, open woodland allowed a multitude of spring flowers to carpet the ground, providing nectar for butterflies and other insects. Such woods were havens for many birds and mammals. Indeed, some woods are coppiced commercially today, and these are rich in wildlife.

As in any habitat, death and decay play important roles in a wood. Fallen leaves are broken down by fungi to form a rich layer of leaf mould, which returns plant nutrients to the earth. Dead trees and fallen branches become festooned with mosses and lichens, providing shelter for all manner of small creatures.

Hawthorn, a decorative small tree, also supports many creatures

Guelder rose has attractive autumn fruits which are eaten by birds

GARDEN WOODLAND HABITATS

To be successful in supporting a wide range of species, a garden woodland should mimic a coppiced wood, providing the dappled shade that is beloved by many of the most beautiful wildflowers.

A small woodland habitat may consist of just a single tree, a shrubbery, a hedgerow or a woody climber, depending on the space you have available and on your chosen garden style.

BUYING NATIVE TREES, SHRUBS AND CLIMBERS

Many common varieties of natives, such as silver birch, hawthorn and ivy, can be bought at garden centres and from general mail-order suppliers. For a greater variety, try specialist nurseries and suppliers.

Container-grown plants can be bought as large specimens for instant effect and can be planted at any time of year. It is much cheaper to buy bare-rooted plants, however, especially if several are needed. Bare-rooted plants are grown in the ground, then dug up before being sold. They must be planted immediately, and their planting period is limited to between autumn and spring. Good bargains are available for buying in bulk, which is particularly useful for hedging.

In practice, it is better to buy younger, smaller plants. These establish and grow away much more quickly, often overtaking a larger, container-grown specimen. Seedling trees and shrubs are also less likely to require staking.

Bonsai nurseries are a useful source of seedlings. Their price lists include one- and two-year old seedlings of various native species, with many common varieties costing around £1 or less. These are normal varieties, not dwarfs, and will grow to full size if allowed.

If you buy plants from a local garden centre or nursery, inspect them carefully to ensure that they are in good condition. Leaves, if present, should look fresh and not be discoloured or shrivelled. There should be no dead or diseased shoots. If container grown, check that the plants are not pot-bound, with the main roots growing out of the base of the container. If bare rooted, the root system should be well developed, with no sign of shrivelling.

Mail-order plants are generally dispatched in excellent condition: the company's reputation depends on this.

Beware of the pre-packaged shrubs and climbers in plastic bags that are available in many supermarkets and hardware shops. The warm conditions in these stores encourage premature growth, and the shrubs need to be hardened off gradually before being planted out in their permanent positions. In my experience, they can be difficult to establish.

Specialist plant suppliers advertise in popular gardening magazines, and most will send a catalogue or price list if requested.

GROWING TREES AND SHRUBS FROM SEEDS

If you're not in a hurry it can be interesting – and surprisingly easy – to grow trees and shrubs from seeds, either bought or collected. This is a cheap way of experimenting with different varieties.

The seeds of trees and shrubs are less readily available than those of seedlings and young plants, but some of the larger seed companies do have a limited selection; check the gardening magazine adverts for any specialist suppliers.

It is enjoyable to collect autumn berries, nuts and other fruits from hedges and trees. Try rose hips, hawthorn haws, ash and field maple keys, acorns, beech masts and anything else you may come across. Isolate the seeds and sow them immediately in small pots or seed trays of compost. Sow more than you need because only a fraction will germinate. Leave them outdoors, in a shady part of the garden, and make sure they don't dry out.

Most varieties take a year, or even two, to germinate, requiring exposure to winter frost for activation. This process may be by-passed by mixing the seeds with damp sand or coir in a plastic bag, then leaving them in the fridge for a few weeks.

When the seedlings are large enough to handle, transfer them to pots and grow them on for a year or two before planting them in their permanent positions.

Occasionally a self-sown seedling will appear as a garden weed, its seed perhaps dropped by a bird or buried by a squirrel. If required, this can be carefully dug up and transferred to a suitable site.

Virtually no garden, even a tiny one, is too small for a tree. As well as supporting wildlife, a tree adds height and shade, provides an attractive focal point and, surprisingly, can actually make a small garden look larger. A specimen such as hawthorn or holly, if sited at the bottom of the garden, tends to look further away than it actually is. This illusion can also be created by planting a small tree behind shrubs.

With more room, a cluster of three or more small trees can look striking. These could be of the same variety – silver birches, for example, are effective when several are planted close together – or different varieties, grouped for contrast.

GROWING TREES AND SHRUBS FROM CUTTINGS AND LAYERING

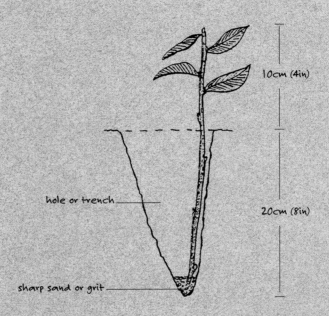

10cm (4in)

hole or trench

20cm (8in)

sharp sand or grit

Plant hardwood cuttings in a deep hole or trench

Many woody plants root easily from hardwood cuttings taken in autumn. Unlike seeds, cuttings always produce plants exactly like the parent. Cut off sections, about 30cm (12in) long, from the ends of the shoots, remove any leaves from the bottom two-thirds, and insert the twigs into a 20cm (8in) deep hole or trench. If your soil is poorly drained, put a layer of sharp sand or grit in the bottom. The cuttings should be well rooted and ready to move to their permanent positions by the following autumn.

Alternatively, semi-ripe cuttings can be taken in early summer. This method tends to work better for conifers and ornamental varieties. Take cuttings 10–15cm (4–6in) long. Remove the leaves from the lower half, dip the twig ends in hormone rooting powder, then insert the cuttings into a pot or tray of gritty compost. Cover with a plastic bag or place in a propagator, then leave outdoors in a shady place. Hardy trees and shrubs do not like being inside or in a heated propagator, but root perfectly well outside, in a shady place, from late spring to early summer.

I have had success with this method, rooting cuttings of a variety of trees and shrubs, including conifers. The cuttings normally root within a few weeks. Pot them up, and plant them out when they have developed a good root system.

Layering is a method of propagation used to root flexible stems of shrubs and climbers while they are still attached to the parent plant. This rarely fails, and many shrubs layer themselves naturally whenever a stem rests on the soil.

To layer a shrub, bury a portion of stem, holding it down with a peg or stone. Rooting, which normally takes from six months to a year, can be encouraged by first making a small slit in the stem to be buried; roots will form readily at this wound. Sever the layered shoots from the parent in the autumn and plant them in their new positions, watering in thoroughly.

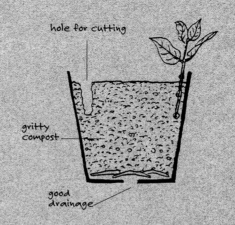

Semi-ripe cuttings can be taken in early summer

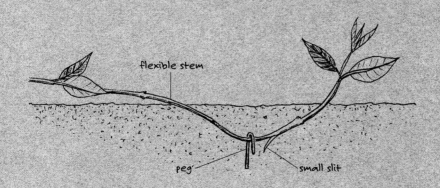

Layering is used to root flexible woody stems still attached to the parent plant

Requiring a little more upkeep, a shrubbery, coppiced tree, or mixed hedgerow will extend the range of species you can grow considerably. Bare walls, fences and internal trellis screens can be clothed with woody climbers and ramblers of woodland edges and clearings.

Whichever style of woodland habitat you choose, the scavengers and decomposers of the food chain can be accommodated by mulching the ground beneath with leaf litter or bark chippings, or arranging a log pile in a shady corner.

See Table 2.1
Page 51

SMALL TREES

There is a good selection of trees suitable for most gardens, even diminutive ones. Many small native trees produce blossoms in spring or early summer, followed by colourful fruits which provide food for birds and small mammals in the winter.

Maples make excellent garden trees, having colourful autumn foliage and attractive fruit, like bunches of keys

Bear in mind the tree's eventual height, spread and shape. In a small garden every plant must earn its space, so choose a variety with colourful blossom or fruit. For winter interest, consider an evergreen or something with coloured bark and twigs. Varieties with purple, golden or variegated foliage are just as valuable to wildlife as are the green-leaved wild types.

The most valuable small native tree for supporting wildlife is hawthorn. It has almost 150 dependent insect species feeding on its leaves or the nectar from its pungent May blossom, and the dense, prickly branches provide safe nesting sites for birds. The deep red autumn haws, so attractive to us, can be life-savers for birds during harsh weather. As well as the common, white-flowered form, hawthorns with red and pink blooms are available.

Red-flowered hawthorn, as well as providing food and shelter for wildlife, is an attractive, decorative plant

Crab apple is another very useful tree, with pink blossoms appearing in spring, followed by miniature apples. Crab apple's nectar and flowers support over 90 insect species, and this is in addition to the birds and mammals that eat the nutritious apples.

Holly is a handsome evergreen. It is available in numerous forms, many variegated, which differ in leaf shape and colour, growth habit and berry colour. There are many good, compact varieties, all of which make excellent nesting sites for birds. The berries, borne only by female plants, can be red, orange or yellow and last from September through most of the winter. They are an important food source for thrushes and other resident birds, for migrants such as fieldfares and redwings, and for the occasional hungry rodent. Holly blue butterflies lay their eggs on the small white flowers in May.

PLANTING TREES AND SHRUBS

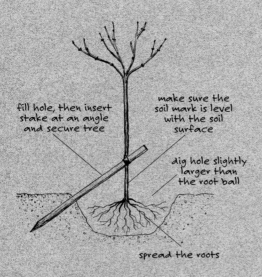

fill hole, then insert stake at an angle and secure tree

make sure the soil mark is level with the soil surface

dig hole slightly larger than the root ball

spread the roots

Bare-rooted trees and shrubs are planted when dormant, in autumn or winter. Taller trees need staking

Trees and shrubs are long-term garden residents so it is important to prepare their planting sites really well. Because the roots will spread, an area of several square metres per tree should be prepared, depending on the eventual size of the plant (the roots tend to spread below ground as far as the branches do above ground).

A month before planting, double dig the area. Remove a spade's depth of soil from one end of the site and put it in a heap at the far end. Fork the subsoil, adding organic material like compost or rotted manure. If the soil is heavy and drainage is poor, add horticultural grit – one bucketful per square metre (yard). Remove another spade's depth of soil from alongside this trench, placing it in the first trench, and continue thus along the area to be dug. Fill the final trench with the soil from the first. (See the illustration, right.) For hedges, double dig a trench at least 60cm (2ft) wide, and add compost or manure.

Soil for climbers needs to be particularly well prepared: there is a tendency for soil next to a fence or wall to become dry as it is sheltered from rain whenever the wind blows from behind the wall. Climbers should be planted at least 30cm (1ft) out from the supporting structure, where at least some rain will reach the roots.

October is best for bare-rooted plants, but planting can be done at any time during winter. Container-grown specimens can be planted at any time of year, but if they are planted in the spring, they will need to be kept well watered in their first summer.

Before planting, container-grown plants must be watered well, and the roots of bare-rooted specimens must first be soaked.

To plant, dig a hole or trench larger than the root ball. Insert the plant, spreading out the roots of non-container plants. Make sure the depth is correct: planting too deep may cause the trunk to rot. For container-grown plants, the top of the compost should be level with the soil surface. Bare-rooted plants should have a soil mark on the stem, indicating the depth at which they were originally planted; this mark should be level with the soil surface.

Mix the removed soil with a couple of handfuls of bone meal or other high phosphate plant food, to encourage root growth, then fill in the hole, shaking the plant gently to remove any air pockets. The fine roots which take water and nutrients from the soil must be in contact with it or they will dry up and die. Shaking a tree or shrub while filling its planting hole with soil ensures that soil falls into all the gaps amongst the roots, so that few or no air pockets remain. The plant will also be better anchored in the ground. Water in well.

Hedge plants should be set 45cm (18in) apart. Planting in a staggered double row will produce a denser hedge.

Larger trees need staking. Use a short stake with a tie near the bottom of the trunk. This will hold the roots firm but allow the tree to move with the wind as it grows and hence become strong and pliant.

Hedging and climbers should have the upper third of their shoots removed after planting to promote dense branching.

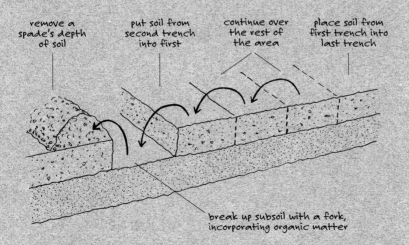

remove a spade's depth of soil

put soil from second trench into first

continue over the rest of the area

place soil from first trench into last trench

break up subsoil with a fork, incorporating organic matter

Preparing the soil for planting by double digging

After the initial watering in, try to avoid watering native trees and shrubs unless the following summer is very dry. Watering encourages shallow roots to develop, which makes the plant susceptible to drought. If left unwatered, the roots will grow deep in search of ground water.

If watering is necessary, flood the surrounding soil well, letting the water soak deeply into the ground. The worst thing to do is water frequently and lightly, as this will encourage surface rooting.

Grass and other ground plants should be kept from growing within 30cm (12in) of the bases of newly planted specimens for the first two years; applying a mulch of biodegradable card or covering the area with a sheet of plastic topped with bark chippings or leaf mould will keep weeds down.

Other than this, native trees and shrubs require little attention. An annual autumn or spring mulch with leaf mould, shredded prunings or bark, when the soil is moist, will provide all the feeding they need.

CONIFERS

When considering trees that are suitable for wildlife, we should not overlook conifers. Although often considered to be of limited use in attracting wildlife, native conifers do, in fact, provide shelter and food for a number of creatures.

It is a common misconception that conifer woods are bad for wildlife while deciduous woods are good. A well-managed conifer plantation, containing trees of different ages, is often richer biologically than are many beech woods.

Conifers are primitive plants, mostly evergreen, with narrow, tough, wax-coated leaves, inedible to many small creatures. A number of insects do feed on conifers, however. The larvae of pine shoot moths, for instance, tunnel into the terminal leaves of pines, while webber moth caterpillars feed on juniper leaves, spinning them together with fine webbing. Adelgids, small sap-suckers related to aphids, feed on the stems and foliage of pine and spruce, producing tufts of white, waxy wool for protection. Conspicuous galls on the young shoots of yew are the work of yew gall midge larvae. Scale insects can encrust the stems of yew and juniper, and mites may attack cypress and spruce. These small herbivores are not generally a problem, as they are kept under control by natural predators.

Many conifers bear woody cones, some conspicuous and decorative. On dry days, the cone segments open up to expose oval, nutty seeds, each with a papery wing, which are dispersed by wind. Some seed-eating birds enjoy a meal of conifer seeds, hanging on to ripe cones and extracting them with their beaks. Squirrels and other rodents also eat conifer seeds. Juniper and yew produce fleshy, berry-like fruits which are actually modified cones. The black or blue fruits of juniper and the red berries of yew are enjoyed by many winter birds.

As well as food, conifers provide dense, evergreen shelter for birds and other creatures. For exposed sites, an excellent shelter belt tree is the mountain pine, a dwarf, gnarled conifer which looks older than it is. This makes an interesting specimen tree, or plant several together for impact.

COPPICED SHRUBS

An interesting way of cultivating trees in a small to medium-sized garden is to practise the ancient art of coppicing. This extends considerably the range of trees that can be grown: regular pruning means that forest trees which are normally huge can be kept to a manageable size.

Many varieties of tree will stand this treatment. Indeed, trees like beech, hornbeam and oak, which grow very large when left untended, are widely used as hedgerow plants in gardens, trimmed regularly to keep them neat and bushy. English oak, the most valuable native tree for growing in this way, is practically a complete habitat in itself, providing food and shelter for over 280 invertebrate species – many of them specific to oak – as well as birds and mammals. An amazing

This alder woodland is managed by coppicing which has wildlife as well as commercial benefits

COPPICING

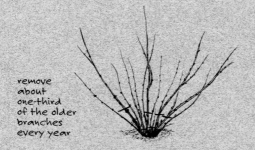

remove about one-third of the older branches every year

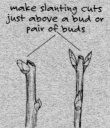

make slanting cuts just above a bud or pair of buds

Trees and shrubs can be kept in check by removing one-third of the branches, along with any dead or diseased wood, every year. Use sharp secateurs, and make sloping cuts just above a bud or buds

Shrubs grown for winter stem colour, such as dogwood and willow, and fast-growing, late-flowering garden shrubs, like buddleia, should be cut back annually to keep them from growing too large. This pruning should be done in March or April, cutting the entire shrub back to around 30cm (12in) in height. It is neater, for a small shrub, to cut just above a bud or pair of buds. The cuts should slope, as opposed to being at right angles to the branch, in order to prevent water collecting on the cut where it may cause rot. The actual angle is not crucial. New shoots will grow rapidly from the old wood.

Less regular coppicing, once every few years as required, can also be used to keep other bushes in check. Winter is a good time for pruning deciduous trees which, if necessary, can be cut back quite severely to 45–60cm (18–24in) in height. Varieties which keep their dried leaves in winter (beech, oak, hornbeam) can be left until spring, after leaf drop.

Alternately, if you prefer, cut back half or one-third of the older branches every year. This is a useful method for slower-growing varieties such as oak and beech, and does not leave a gap while they are growing back. It is best to cut single specimens manually, using secateurs or a pruning saw.

The prunings can be used as plant supports or firewood, or can be shredded and used as mulching material.

Naturally small trees or shrubs do not need pruning, except to remove any dead or infected shoots that appear.

variety of nibbling, mining and sap-sucking insects feed from its leaves, including caterpillars of the oak roller and tortrix moths, which roll up leaves into small tubes in order to hide themselves from hungry bluetits and tree sparrows.

When selecting a tree for coppicing avoid non-natives, such as sycamore, horse and sweet chestnuts, and Japanese cherries: these support relatively few insect species.

Vigorous coppiced trees, like ash, require annual pruning to keep them in check. Slow growers, such as oak and beech, can be trimmed every few years, or have some of their older branches removed annually.

See Table 2.2
Page 53

HEDGEROWS

Planting a hedge made up of native species is an excellent way of introducing a woodland-edge habitat which does not take up much space.

The most ancient of Britain's hedgerows were planted around 1,000 years ago, to mark Saxon boundaries. They are rich in plant life; a collection of hawthorn and field maple, mixed with guelder rose, blackthorn, holly and wild privet. Most hedges are relatively

Commonly used as a hedging plant, oak retains its dried leaves in winter

Hawthorn is a useful hedging shrub for wildlife

modern, however, being 'only' around 200 years old. These were planted as boundaries when common land was carved up and sold off.

Over the decades, these hedges have become important wildlife corridors, allowing the migration and spread of plants and animals over many miles. Herbaceous plants of woodland clearings established themselves along verges and hedge bottoms, and birds nested among the dense and tangled twigs.

The loss of tens of thousands of miles of hedgerows has received much publicity. In Britain, the Countryside Survey, 1990, carried out over a period of 12 years, revealed that a quarter of rural hedgerows vanished between 1984 and 1990. With this decline of hedgerows in the countryside, private gardens are important conservation sites for hedges and their dependent wildlife.

Hedges are easy to plant and maintain and, in the long term, are far cheaper to keep than fences as they are less likely to blow down, do not fall into disrepair and will never

PRUNING MIXED HEDGES

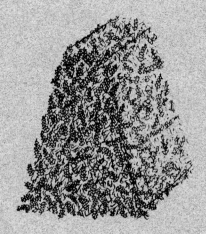

Hedges, whether formal or informal, should be wider at the base than the top. This allows light to reach the lower branches

Mixed hedgerows are most interesting if they are allowed to grow quite untidy, with the shrubs merging to form a dense, informal barrier.

The individual varieties in a mixed hedge grow at different rates, so pruning is slightly more complicated than with a single-species hedge. Take care not to disturb nesting birds or remove any flowers or winter berries and nuts.

Pruning is generally required once or twice a year. Late winter is a good time, after the birds have eaten all the haws, hips and other fruit. Cut straggly branches well back and shorten the rest, using secateurs, a pruning saw, or a power pruner. The hedge can also be tidied in late summer, after any nestlings have left; cut back any vigorous branches, then clip with hand shears or a power pruner.

Strongly growing species, such as field maple and hawthorn, may need more frequent pruning to prevent them from smothering the more timid varieties.

A hedge should be cut so that it is narrower at its top than at its base. This shape allows light to reach all the way down to the base of the hedge, promoting dense growth to ground level. It also reduces the risk of snow settling on top and distorting the shape or breaking branches.

need replacing. A delightful alternative to the ubiquitous common privet or Leyland cypress (x *Cupressocyparis leylandii*), a native hedgerow may contain just one type of shrub or, more valuable and interesting, a mixture. Many trees and shrubs are suitable for hedging, including all those that can be grown as coppiced shrubs and several small tree varieties including blackthorn, elder, field maple, guelder rose, hawthorn, holly and yew.

WOODY CLIMBERS

If you really have no room for a tree, coppiced shrub or hedge, it is still possible to create a woodland habitat; a native climber can fulfil most of the functions of trees and shrubs. They take up little space horizontally, and can decorate a boundary fence, internal screen or the house walls, providing shelter for birds, beasts and insects. Climbers and ramblers are plants with weak, fast-growing stems which depend on bushes or trees for support. Several are common woodland edge plants, also found in hedgerows.

See Table 2.3 Page 54

Honeysuckle is a beautiful native climber

Blackbirds like to nest among the tangled stems of climbers such as clematis

Native climbers support a large variety of wild creatures. Indeed some of them, particularly honeysuckle and ivy, are amongst the most valuable plants for attracting wildlife into the garden. Blackbirds, wrens and many other garden birds like to nest among the tangled stems of dense climbers such as ivy, honeysuckle and clematis. Their flowers provide pollen and nectar for countless insects, while their fruits are life-savers for birds and small mammals in winter. The leaves and even the bark are also put to use by various creatures. Strips of peeling bark from old honeysuckle, for example, are used by many species of birds as nest-building material.

As well as being useful, native climbers and ramblers are attractive plants. Many rival their more exotic garden cousins in the beauty of their flowers and fruits. There is also a good and varied selection: some, for example honeysuckle and wild roses, produce scented blossoms, which attract night moths, in summer; many, including roses and brambles, have colourful and nutritious autumn fruits and one, ivy, is evergreen.

It is a myth that climbers cause damage to brickwork. Providing that the wall is in good condition, ivy and other climbers will actually work to protect it from harsh weather conditions and to provide a layer of insulation for a house.

Some climbers, including ivy, are self-clinging, but most need support. If wires, netting or a trellis are secured a few centimetres from the wall, the gap behind them will keep the wall dry; it will also be used as a hiding place by nesting birds, hibernating insects and, perhaps, roosting bats. Such a gap can be created easily by fixing wooden blocks to the wall and attaching the support to these.

This colourful butterfly, a painted lady, is taking a rest on the stem of a spiny bramble bush

WOODLAND FLOOR PLANTS

Once your tree, shrub, hedge or climber is established, the dry, dappled shade beneath provides the perfect environment for woodland wildflowers. There is a huge variety, with most blooming in spring before the trees come into leaf and block out the sunlight. As well as cheering people up after the winter gloom, these wildflowers are important providers of nectar and pollen for early butterflies like the comma, orange-tip, white admiral and speckled wood.

In a small space, keep to smaller, less invasive woodland flowers. Evergreen creepers, such as ivy and lesser periwinkle, also grow well in woodland conditions, providing excellent ground cover in which molluscs, insects and amphibians can hide.

See Table 2.4 Page 55

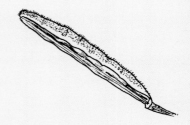

Caterpillar of orange-tip butterfly camouflaged against a seed pod of garlic mustard; these larvae feed on only four plant species

Many of the common woodland wild-flowers may be bought as young plants or bulbs from specialist nurseries and garden centres. They can also be grown from seeds, which are often available in mixed packets. Sow seeds in small pots and leave them outdoors over winter to germinate the following spring.

LEAF LITTER

For your woodland habitat to be complete, an additional factor should be included: decay. As described in Chapter 1, decay and decomposition are needed to recycle the component materials of dead things and return them to the soil and air. In woods this process takes place mainly in the leaf mould on the ground and the dead wood of fallen branches and trees.

Daffodils grow under trees and shrubs in spring, before the leaf canopy blocks the sunlight

Incorporating leaves into a garden woodland is easy; they can just be left on the soil where they fall. The annual shedding of leaves from trees is part of the natural cycle of a wood. Over a few months the leaves will be broken down by the action of microbes, fungi and scavengers, eventually forming a rich, organic leaf mould that feeds and conditions the soil.

Many gardeners still burn fallen leaves in the autumn, not realizing that they are destroying one of the richest wildlife habitats. Leaf litter provides food and shelter for a multitude of creatures. It has been estimated that $1m^3$ ($35ft^3$) of beech litter contains 320,000 mites, 51,000 springtails, and numerous other invertebrates including nematodes, slugs and snails, woodlice, millipedes, roundworms, bristletails and beetle grubs, and countless bacteria, soil amoebae and other microbes. These little scavengers feed on fallen leaves, helping to convert them into humus and plant nutrients. Due to their large surface area to volume ratio, there is a danger of them drying out. Because of this, many have waxy coatings and excrete their nitrogenous waste in a dry state so that little moisture is lost.

In turn, these creatures are preyed upon by carnivores including centipedes, false scorpions, spiders and harvestmen. All of them are eaten by blackbirds and thrushes, which can often be seen rustling through leaf litter for morsels.

Leaf litter is also broken down by ground fungi. Their colourful fruiting bodies appear in autumn when the weather is damp but still warm. These are nibbled by the larvae and adults of many insects, including boletus and fungus beetles.

Draparnaud's snail is carnivorous, eating insect larvae

As well as mimicking nature by leaving leaves on the ground beneath shrubs and trees, you could also pile dead leaves in a sheltered spot where hedgehogs and other small mammals can burrow under them for their winter hibernation.

Trees like this alder are a good framework for spiders' webs

DEAD WOOD

The second type of woodland decay habitat, dead wood, can be introduced into your garden in the form of pruned twigs and logs. These can be piled in a hidden corner, perhaps behind a bushy shrub where they won't be disturbed. Don't hide the pile too well, though: it is interesting to keep an eye on your heap to see what takes up residence.

In a wood, broken branches and fallen trees are slowly attacked by the thread-like mycelia of fungi which spread through the wood, turning it into pulp.

In autumn a variety of toadstools sprout from the mycelia, from tiny pink orbs to large brown brackets, depending on what wood the heap contains.

A pile of decaying logs is home to all sorts of living things

Dead wood also provides a home for many small creatures that spend at least some of their lives eating it or hiding under it. Soon your logs will be drilled with little holes. Many insects and other invertebrates bore into dead wood that has been softened by fungal action. Among these are the larvae of many beetles, including the fat white grubs of the slug-eating lesser stag beetle and small, flying wood wasps which are active throughout the summer, boring tunnels in which to lay their eggs.

As with leaf litter, decaying wood attracts predators to its ready food supply. Garden spiders spin webs to net flies and wood wasps. Small, well-camouflaged hunting spiders, rather than making webs, lurk invisible, ready to pounce on passing prey.

WOODLAND BIRDS AND MAMMALS

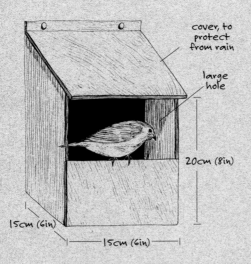

cover, to protect from rain

large hole

20cm (8in)

15cm (6in)

15cm (6in)

Bird boxes encourage birds to nest in your garden. Robins prefer large holes or open boxes near the ground

Woodland habitats can provide homes for many birds and mammals – you can help them even more by providing purpose-built homes.

Birds are attracted to your garden if there are plenty of nesting and roosting sites. Trees, climbers and hedges themselves serve this purpose, but you can encourage even more birds to move in by putting up nest boxes on shady walls, fences and trees. These mimic holes in old trees, which used to be much more common in the countryside.

You can buy nest boxes from the Royal Society for the Protection of Birds (RSPB) and other outlets, or make your own. Different birds prefer entrance holes of different sizes. Tits like very small holes, for example, while robins prefer large holes or open sites nearer ground level. (Bluetits like a hole of about 3cm (1¼in) diameter maximum, great tits need 3.5cm (1½in), and sparrows 5cm (2in). Robins, pied wagtails and spotted flycatchers like a large hole at least 15cm (6in) across, or even an open ledge.) Make sure the boxes are difficult for cats to reach and out of direct sunlight: nest box interiors can get very hot in direct sunlight, which is harmful to eggs and chicks.

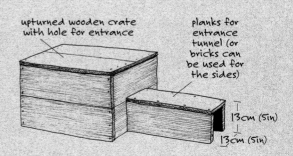

upturned wooden crate with hole for entrance

planks for entrance tunnel (or bricks can be used for the sides)

13cm (5in)

13cm (5in)

A hedgehog hibernation house made out of an upturned wooden crate

Bats roost and hibernate in hollow trees and the roof spaces of old buildings, including barns. These flying mammals are useful insect predators, but some species are endangered because suitable homes are now more difficult to find, so bat boxes are needed even more urgently than bird boxes. They are similar to bird boxes, but with the entrance in the base. Again, these can be bought or made. Set them in a shady spot, 3–5m (10–16ft) above the ground.

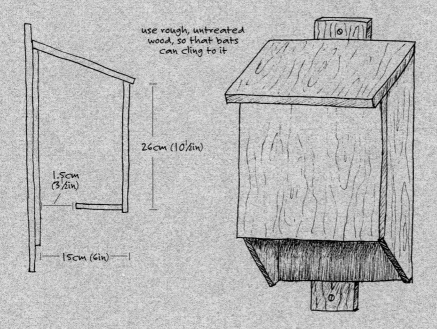

use rough, untreated wood, so that bats can cling to it

26cm (10½in)

1.5cm (3½in)

15cm (6in)

The entrance hole for bats must be at the base of the box

The most useful ground-dwelling mammal in gardens is the hedgehog, which eats slugs and other invertebrates. Hedgehogs need dry, sheltered places in which to hibernate, and often burrow under leaf or twig piles. Even better, you could buy or make a special hibernation house. A simple design using an upturned wooden crate or box is shown in the diagram. Cut a hole for an entrance, and make an entrance tunnel from wooden planks or two rows of bricks with a plank on top. Site your hedgehog house in a shady place where it will not be disturbed – behind shrubs is good – and cover it with fallen leaves to disguise it.

Your woodland habitat may attract small mammals such as woodmice

Cool, damp hollows under the logs shelter moisture-loving creatures. Worms, slugs, snails, springtails, centipedes, millipedes and ground beetles hide here during the day, emerging at night to seek food in the damp vegetation. Adult newts, toads and frogs often shelter in decaying wood in summer, along with small mammals such as wood mice, shrews and hedgehogs. In winter, a pile of woody prunings will prove invaluable to hibernating slow worms, mice and hedgehogs, while clusters of ladybirds await the warming spring sunshine inside hollow twigs.

An alternative to a log pile in a garden is to mulch under shrubs and trees with coarsely shredded prunings or bark. This shelters and feeds many of the creatures of decaying wood, and is more suitable for an ornamental garden.

TABLE 2.1

SMALL NATIVE TREES (continued over page)

Tree	Final height (m)	Final height (ft)	Evergreen	Remarks
Alder buckthorn *Frangula alnus**	5	16	No	Prefers moist, peaty soils. Tiny, green-white flowers followed by berries that mature from green through cherry red to glossy black
Aspen *Populus tremula*	5	16	No	The smallest poplar. Good for windy sites. Its rounded, toothed leaves tremble in the breeze. Yellow autumn foliage
Blackthorn *Prunus spinosa*	5	16	No	Also called sloe. Bushy tree with clouds of white blossom in March before leaves emerge. Small, blue-black plums in autumn. 'Purpurea' has purple leaves
Crab apple *Malus sylvestris*	5–7	16–23	No	Pale pink spring blossom. Miniature apples in autumn. Supports over 90 insect species. Many ornamental varieties
Elder *Sambucus nigra*	8	26	No	Umbels of scented, cream-white flowers in June, attractive to many insects. Shiny black berries in September eaten by a variety of birds. 'Aurea' has golden foliage, 'Purpurea' has purple leaves
Field maple *Acer campestre*	7	23	No	Attractive lobed leaves, pink when young, turning golden in autumn. Avoid the related sycamore (*A. pseudoplatanus*) which is very vigorous and large
Guelder rose *Viburnum opulus*	5	16	No	Prefers moist, limy soil. Heavily scented, flat heads of white flowers in May and June attract night moths. In autumn, its leaves turn crimson and scarlet and its translucent red berries attract migratory birds
Hawthorn *Crataegus monogyna, C. oxyacantha*	5–8	16–26	No	Supports nearly 150 insect species. Clusters of scented, white, pink or red flowers in May. Crimson haws appear in September. *Crataegus oxyacantha* varieties are smaller and less thorny than those of *C. monogyna*

* This was previously known as *Rhamnus frangula*

TABLE 2.1

SMALL NATIVE TREES (continued)

Tree	Final height (m)	Final height (ft)	Evergreen	Remarks
Holly *Ilex aquifolium*	6–8	20–26	Yes	Numerous forms, many variegated. Female varieties produce red, orange or yellow berries which last from September throughout winter. Good for early bird nests. Small white flowers in May
Juniper *Juniperus communis*	3	10	Yes	A shrubby tree that will withstand wind and drought. The blue-black, berry-like fruits are relished by birds in winter. 'Stricta' is grey-blue and of columnar form. Several dwarf forms are available
Mountain ash *Sorbus aucuparia*	8	26	No	White flower clusters in May and June. Clusters of scarlet berries ripen in August. Yellow-fruited forms, eg 'Joseph Rock', lose their berries to feeding birds later in the year. Yellow and orange autumn foliage
Mountain pine *Pinus mugo*	5	16	Yes	A gnarled shrub, suitable for exposed sites. *Pinus mugo pumilo* is a dwarf form, 2m (6½ft) high
Silver birch *Betula pendula*	8	26	No	Fast-growing tree with white, flaking bark. 'Youngii' and 'Tristis' are fine weeping forms, 'Purpurea' has purple leaves and branches. The columnar 'Fastigiata' is ideal for small gardens
Spindle tree *Euonymus europaeus*	4	13	No	Green-white flowers in May, followed by red fruits which open to reveal orange seeds, giving a showy display until eaten by birds. Pink or red autumn foliage. 'Red Cascade' has even showier fruits
Whitebeam *Sorbus aria*	7	23	No	Its leaves are silver-white and downy underneath, turning gold in autumn. Panicles of cream flowers in May and June are followed by bunches of scarlet berries which ripen in September
Yew *Taxus baccata*	5	16	Yes	Slow growing and extremely hardy, withstanding wind and drought. Male and female flowers are borne on separate plants. All parts, except the red flesh of the fruits, are poisonous. 'Aurea' has golden foliage

TABLE 2.2

TREES SUITABLE FOR COPPICING

Tree	Remarks	Pruning
Alder *Alnus glutinosa*	Likes damp soil. 'Aurea' is slower growing and has yellow leaves	As required, in spring
Ash *Fraxinus excelsior*	Good for windy site. Suitable for town and seaside gardens	Annually; use branches as plant supports
Beech *Fagus sylvatica*	Green or copper-red leaves. Small specimens retain their dry, russet leaves in winter	As required, in July
Dogwood *Cornus sanguinea*	Likes chalky soil. Small white flowers. Purple-red stems conspicuous in winter	Annually, in April
Gean or wild cherry *Prunus avium*	White flower clusters in April, small, sweet cherries in late summer	When required, in late summer
Hazel *Corylus avellana*	Good for exposed and coastal sites. Lamb's-tail catkins in spring	As required, in early spring; use prunings as plant supports
Hornbeam *Carpinus betulus*	Retains its dried leaves throughout winter	As required; prunings make good fuel
Oak *Quercus robur*	Supports over 280 insect species. Retains some dried leaves throughout winter	As required, in winter; prunings make good firewood
Privet *Ligustrum vulgare*	White, fragrant flowers in July, black berries in autumn. 'Aureum' has yellow leaves	Annually, in May or August
Pussy willow or sallow *Salix caprea*	Prefers damp soil. Male and female catkins produced on separate plants	As required, in winter
Small-leaved lime *Tilia cordata*	Thrives on deep, loamy soil	As required
White willow *Salix alba*	Needs moist soil; — var. *vitellina* (golden osier) has brilliant yellow winter twigs	Annually

Alder cones

TABLE 2.3

WOODY CLIMBERS

Climber	Evergreen	Remarks
Bramble *Rubus fruticosus*	No	White or pale pink flowers in late spring attract bees, butterflies and other insects. Blackberries appear from mid-August
Clematis *Clematis vitalba*	No	Also called traveller's joy and old man's beard. Cream flowers in July and August, followed by fluffy fruits. Dense, tangled branches shelter nesting birds
Dog rose *Rosa canina*	No	White or pink flowers in June and July. Scarlet hips, popular with birds of the thrush family, ripen in December
Honeysuckle *Lonicera periclymenum*	No	Also called woodbine. Perfumed yellow-and-crimson flowers, appearing from May to July, attract night moths. Strips of old bark used as bird nesting material
Ivy *Hedera helix*	Yes	Dense shelter for nesting birds and hibernating butterflies. Small yellow flowers from October to December. Purple-black fruits in late winter
Woody nightshade *Solanum dulcamara*	No	Also called bittersweet. Bunches of dainty purple-and-yellow flowers in summer. Red berries in autumn, poisonous to humans but relished by birds

Honeysuckle flower

Ivy leaves

TABLE 2.4

WOODLAND FLOOR PLANTS

Plant	Remarks
Bluebell *Endymion non-scripta* *	Clusters of bell flowers in late spring. Spreads well when established
Bugle *Ajuga reptans*	Blue flower spikes attract bees and butterflies
Daffodil *Narcissus pseudonarcissus*	Dwarf native variety, with yellow flowers earlier than those of most cultivated varieties
Foxglove *Digitalis purpurea*	Biennial. Pink or white flower spires up to 2m (6½ft) tall
Herb robert *Geranium robertianum*	Red stems, divided leaves and small pink flowers. Self seeds well
Primrose *Primula vulgaris*	Pale yellow flowers visited by early insects
Red campion *Silene dioica*	Magenta flowers in spring and early summer. Its decorative seed capsules are used in winter by hibernating ladybirds
Snowdrop *Galanthus nivalis*	Early, nodding white flowers visited by bees and other insects for nectar
Stinking hellebore *Helleborus foetidus*	This striking plant produces green flower clusters in early spring
Stinking iris *Iris foetidissima*	Grown mainly for its orange, berry-like seeds, revealed when the seed pods split in late summer. Unusual brown-yellow flowers
Strawberry *Fragaria vesca*	The white flowers of wild strawberry are followed by tiny, sweet fruit in July and August
Violet *Viola riviniana*	Common violet has scentless mauve flowers
Wild arum *Arum maculatum*	Also called lords and ladies. Unusual cream, hood-shaped flower, followed by spike of orange berries
Wood anemone *Anemone nemorosa*	White or pale pink 'wind flowers' from March to May, visited by bees for their pollen

Wild arum

*The genus endymion has been renamed hyacinthoides

PONDS, STREAMS
AND MARSHES

Wetland habitats

An area of water is one of the most important features in a wildlife-friendly garden. Not only does it support an interesting variety of aquatic plants and animals, it also provides vital drinking water – and everything needs to drink. A garden wetland will be visited by birds, mammals, amphibians and insects.

HISTORY

Egyptian gardens of around 1400BC had pools, and Persian and Roman gardens of over 2,000 years ago contained rectangular pools. In Britain, ponds were mainly functional until the end of the Middle Ages, in the mid-fifteenth century. After this time, formal ponds were built in the gardens of some grand houses, and informal gardens with lakes became popular in the mid-eighteenth century.

Until the twentieth century ponds had always been central features of country life. Every village, farm and manor estate had at least one pond, and often several for different purposes. As well as being useful to the villagers and farmers, these ponds also became important habitats for a large number of native plants and animals.

Ponds and lakes may form when a river becomes dammed or changes its course, or when a low area is flooded by ground water; very few country ponds are natural, however. The word 'pond' is derived from the same Anglo-Saxon word as 'pound', meaning animal enclosure. Our ancestors dug ponds, or 'enclosures for water', wherever needed, in villages, farmland and pasture. More recently, quarries and excavation sites have been allowed to flood when the work there has been finished.

PONDS AND COUNTRY LIFE

Village ponds used to be vital for everyday life and local industries. As well as providing domestic water and drinking water for animals, many ponds were stocked with fish. Manor houses and monasteries had special ponds in which fish were farmed for eating.

Ponds and their banks were sources of clay and willow wands for wattle-and-daub house walls. Clay from ponds was also used for pottery, and spread on sandy fields to improve the soil. Rushes from pond margins were used for thatching and lighting.

Our ancestors made a country pond by digging a hole in the lowest part of a field or village green, lining it with clay, then driving cattle over it to compress and make it waterproof. They sometimes added flints to provide a firm footing for animals wading into the shallows to drink.

In England, canal building began in earnest after the start of the Industrial Revolution in the late eighteenth century, and a network of canals was rapidly built. This was used for the transport of goods until World War I, but is now used mainly for leisure. The canals, which are like long, narrow ponds, have developed into important corridors for wetland wildlife.

Once there were over 350,000 ponds in England and Wales, but most of these were lost during the twentieth century due to neglect, increased extraction from water tables, or because the land was required for other purposes. Ponds are unstable and, left to themselves, will gradually silt up to become first marsh, then dry land colonized by willow, alder or birch. Many country ponds have been filled in or drained to be used for farmland or for building developments. Those that remain are often polluted with fertilizer run-off or agrochemicals, harming the wildlife which inhabits them.

It is not just lakes and ponds that are at risk; natural marshes and swamps, once extensive throughout Britain, are becoming increasingly endangered by the effects of drainage and pollution. Over the last 50 years, more than half of Britain's lowland fens have been lost.

Country ponds and marshes are now rare

Not only do these habitats support some of the most beautiful and rare wildflowers, they also provide valuable cover for amphibians and other creatures.

Freshwater ecology, developed over centuries, is complex and easily damaged. Wetlands are particularly susceptible to pollution, both from industrial effluent and heavily fertilized or manured agricultural land; a build-up of certain minerals can inhibit plant growth. Due to the loss of and damage to much of these habitats, many wetland plants and animals are in danger of extinction. The common frog, for instance, has decreased in numbers by 90% over the last 30 years and has probably been saved only by the growing number of ponds in gardens and smallholdings.

GARDEN WETLAND HABITATS

There is a wide range of types and styles of wetland habitats, providing something to suit most gardens. These habitats include pools, streams, canals and marshes, alone or in combination. Although formal water features can still support wildlife, informal ones look more natural.

An important consideration for attracting wildlife is whether to have still or running water. Both have their advantages and disadvantages, and the species they support are different.

Blue damselflies may visit your garden wetland

Since gas diffusion is slower in water than in air, and oxygen is not readily soluble in water, still water can easily become stagnant. This problem can usually be overcome by planting submerged pond weeds because they release oxygen into the water as they photosynthesize. On a sunny day, evidence of this can be seen, with small streams of oxygen bubbles emanating from submerged aquatic plants. Fountains will also aerate water, but they hardly look natural in a wildlife pool.

Shallow, flowing water can be fully aerated, but it is difficult for some plants and animals to gain a hold on the bottom. In a very fast stream, even silt on the bottom is washed away and only simple plants like algae can survive, sheltered in rock crevices. A stream flowing into a pool, perhaps through a waterfall, is an excellent, natural-looking way of aerating the water. Plants with flexible stems, rooted among rocks or in mud, can survive slower-moving water.

A small marshland looks good next to, or surrounding, a pond or stream, providing a natural transition between water and land. It is a useful and attractive habitat in its own right, however, and can stand alone. If you have young children, it is a safer alternative to a pool.

Small versions of this bulrush are available for garden ponds

PONDS

Ponds are the simplest and most popular type of garden water feature. There is an enormous choice of style, shape and size, some better than others for supporting wildlife. Since it is impossible to move a pond once it is dug and filled, it is important to plan carefully before making one.

An irregularly shaped pond looks most natural. If you prefer a formal style, however, a geometric shape – circle, oval, square, rectangle or polygon – may suit the garden better, and the wildlife won't notice the difference.

If at all possible, your pond should be level with or slightly lower than the ground to enable ease of access for wildlife. Owners of paved yards, balconies and roof gardens may have no choice but to have a raised pond; this will still be accessible to birds and flying insects, but mammals and amphibians will be unable to visit.

CONVERTING A POND FOR WILDLIFE

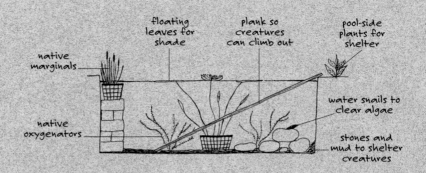

floating
leaves for
shade

plank so
creatures
can climb out

pool-side
plants for
shelter

native
marginals

native
oxygenators

water snails to
clear algae

stones and
mud to shelter
creatures

A formal or prefabricated pond can easily be made more wildlife friendly

If you already have a pond, but it is not an ideal shape or style for wildlife, it is possible to make it more wildlife friendly. The first step is to remove any fish, which tend to eat most small wildlife. If you want to keep fish, you should use a separate pond for this.

If there are no shelves for marginals, pile bricks against the sides to support pots of native marsh plants.

A pond can be too clean. If necessary, add a little soil and some smooth stones to the bottom to provide shelter for a range of pond creatures. Make sure there is sufficient oxygenating weed.

If the sides are steep, even vertical, you will need to provide shallow water and an escape route for frogs and other creatures. A pile of smooth rocks against the edge will do. Alternatively, a sloping plank of wood can be propped against the edge.

At least part of the pond's edge should be gently sloping: this allows pond animals, and any visitors who venture too far, to climb out. In addition, birds enjoy bathing in shallow water – in fact, it is necessary for keeping their plumage in good condition.

You could include shelves at various depths to take pots of water plants. It is generally recommended that part of a pond should be at least 45–60cm (18–24in) deep to avoid the water freezing totally in winter, but this may not be possible in a very small pond.

Your pond size depends on the room you have available and on your overall garden design and requirements. Larger pools are more ecologically balanced and need less looking after, but the tiniest ponds are still valuable for attracting wildlife.

Red damselflies are common visitors to garden ponds

Siting a pond is very important. Choose a low-lying spot like the bottom of a slope, if you have one. So saying, it is hard, messy work digging boggy ground, so if the low spot of your garden is poorly drained, it might be easier to choose a higher site. Of course, a hole in wet ground may fill naturally from ground water and require no liner.

Avoid overhanging trees as they will drop leaves and foul the water. Furthermore, their roots may be damaged during the excavation of the hole. An open, sunny but sheltered spot is best. This will allow the submerged plants to photosynthesize well and keep the water aerated and fresh.

A pond with its wildlife is so attractive and interesting you will want it to be visible either from the house or from a garden seat or summer house. If it is near a building, you could direct rainwater from the guttering into it to keep it topped up.

Choosing a pond liner

These days most modern garden ponds are made with a flexible plastic liner. There is a range of materials to suit various requirements and budgets, from cheap, short-lived black polythene to the more expensive butyl rubber, which is guaranteed to last 10 years or more. Flexible liners can be used for most shapes, sizes and styles.

See Table 3.1 Page 80

The other popular pond liner is pre-formed rigid plastic or fibreglass. These cost more than flexible liners, but are light and easy to install and ideal for small water features. Again, various shapes and sizes are available. Before flexible and pre-formed liners were available most garden ponds were made of concrete, and this is still a cheap and versatile

MAKING A POND WITH A FLEXIBLE LINER

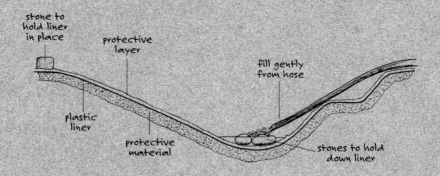

stone to
hold liner
in place

protective
layer

fill gently
from hose

plastic
liner

protective
material

stones to hold
down liner

Making a pond with a flexible liner

For a small pond it is easier, and looks better, to make the shape simple: oval, kidney, figure-of-eight or pear, for example. Mark the outline by sticking canes in the ground at intervals, or laying down rope or a flexible hose pipe.

Dig the hole, making it 15cm (6in) larger than required at the bottom and sides. At least one side should have a gentle slope and, preferably, one part should be at least 45cm (18in) deep, unless the pond is very small. You can include shelves at suitable depths for pots of aquatic and marginal plants.

Check that the edge is level by placing a plank of wood across the hole, lengthways then widthways, and testing with a spirit level. Remove any stones and other hard objects from the soil, then firm the ground.

Line the hole with a protective layer; sand, old carpet, thick newspaper or damp cardboard are all suitable. The dimensions of the lining need to be those of the pond, plus twice the maximum depth, and an extra 30cm (12in) for overlap. So, a pond of 180 x 240cm (70 x 95in), with a maximum depth of 45cm (18in) requires a liner of (180 + (2 x 45) + 30) x (240 + (2 x 45) + 30)cm, that is, 300 x 360cm (118 x 408in).

Spread the liner and let it sag into the hole under its own weight. Anchor the edge by placing bricks or similar heavy objects at intervals around it.

You can fill the pond with water at this point; however, it is a good idea to add a protective layer of polyester matting, old carpet or underlay on top of the liner, and then to sprinkle this with sieved soil. This protects the liner from the sun's rays – plastic lining breaks down when exposed to ultraviolet rays – and physical damage, camouflages it, making the pond look more natural, and provides a rooting medium for aquatic plants. You could place a few rounded stones on the bottom to provide shelter for small creatures.

Now you are ready to fill the pond. Rainwater is best, but it's unlikely you'll have anywhere near enough stored to fill even a small pond. Tap water, via a hose pipe, is fine for filling a new pond. To avoid disturbing the soil layer, place the hose end on a piece of matting or plastic at the edge and let the water trickle in gently. It can take considerable time to fill a pond.

The pressure of the water will hold the liner in place, but its edges will need to be covered. Paving stones, rounded rocks, turf or soil can all be used for this. Part of the shore should be planted with dense shrubs or ground cover to encourage shy creatures to approach.

The flexible liner used for this pond is invisible, covered with pebbles, stones and turf

PRE-FORMED RIGID LINERS

These are light and easy to install. Just dig a hole to fit the contours, firm the ground and drop in the pool, checking that the rim is level. If your ground is stony, you may prefer to line the hole with sand or old newspaper before inserting the liner: even a small pond is very heavy when filled with water, and the pressure of a filled pond on stone can eventually damage the liner.

Rigid pond liners usually have shelves for submerged pots of water plants, but the sides may be too steep for creatures to climb out easily. A pile of large stones on one of the ledges will provide an exit route.

Hide the pond edges with paving slabs, rounded stones or turf.

option. It is best to insert a reinforcing mesh to prevent the concrete cracking under pressure as it settles. Fresh concrete can also secrete toxic chemicals into the water, so the inside should be coated with an insulating paint and the water changed after one month before you introduce any pond life.

You could line your pond with puddled clay. The traditional way of lining ponds was to spread wet clay over the inside of the excavation and then drive a herd of cows over the clay to compact it and hence make it waterproof. These days, people walking over the clay can do the same job – a messy task, but fun for children. Most country ponds, canals and reservoirs were, and still are, made in this way. Plants can root directly into the clay and the edge will blend easily and naturally into the surroundings.

CANALS AND MOATS

Interesting variations for garden water features, including miniature canals and moats, can be created. Although the real things were man-made, to provide a means of transport or protection, both of these wetland habitats and their banks were quickly colonized, and today are valuable wildlife habitats in both town and country.

Canals in the garden are not a new idea. Centuries, even millennia ago, in Mediterranean and Middle Eastern countries, straight canals in formal gardens were popular. Large European country gardens copied this idea, perhaps the greatest being the Grand Canal

MAKING A CONCRETE POND

Concrete ponds are best made in autumn or winter in order to allow the concrete to mature and the water to clear before introducing pond life.

Dig the hole and make sure the ground is firm enough to support the pond. The edges should be gently sloping, not only for ease of exit for wildlife, but also to reduce the risk of the concrete cracking under pressure if the pond surface freezes; the expanding ice sheet will ride up the sides rather than putting pressure on them. Include submerged shelves if you wish.

Add the concrete as quickly as possible to avoid it setting unevenly. A 10cm (4in) layer is needed. Use a mixture of one part Portland cement, two parts sand, and three parts gravel or aggregate. Alternatively, small bags of ready-mixed concrete can be bought from water garden centres. Whichever you use, mix it up with water and a concrete waterproofing liquid to make a stiff dough. Spread this thickly in the hole, making sure that the edges are level. Unless the pond is very small, it is a good idea to strengthen the concrete by incorporating a reinforcing mesh such as chicken wire or nylon netting. To do this, spread a layer of concrete in the hole, place a layer of chicken wire or nylon netting on the wet concrete and press it in lightly, then spread a further concrete layer on top to hide the mesh.

Pebbles or gravel can be pushed into the wet concrete around the perimeter of the pond to hide the edge.

Concrete is very alkaline, a condition which is toxic to living things, so when it has set, paint the surface with a proprietary, waterproof sealing paint. These are available in various colours, from bright blue to neutral, and reduce the leaching of lime from concrete.

Fill the pond with water, empty it after a month to remove any dissolved toxic substances, then refill. It should then be safe to plant up your pool.

Concrete waterproofing liquids and pond-sealing paints are available from specialist water garden centres.

in the Renaissance garden at Versailles. Many grand country houses were fully or partly surrounded by moats, as much for decoration as defence.

A canal is a long, narrow pond. In a garden, if the ground is level, it can be used to give a similar effect to a stream, but it is much simpler to make because no pump is needed. It

MAKING A CLAY-LINED POND

Dig the hole as described in Making a pond with a flexible liner (see page 64). If your soil is naturally heavy clay, you may not need to import any. In this case, follow the process for powdered clay, given below.

The easiest way to make a clay pond is to use Bentonite lining membrane, which consists of clay granules between two membranes; it has the advantage of being suitable for large or irregularly shaped ponds because it is easy to join membrane edges to make a waterproof seal. It also self-heals when punctured.

To prevent worms and other creatures from burrowing through the clay, first dress the surface of the hole with soot, ash or lime – worms seem to find these materials irritating and avoid them.

Bentonite lining is laid in a similar way to plastic liners (see Making a pond with a flexible liner, page 64). Dig a trench around the pond or canal, 30cm (12in) deep and wide, and anchor the edges into this. Make sure that the rolls of material run down the slopes, not across them, and overlap any join by 15cm (6in). Cover the membrane with 20cm (8in) of soil or clay, and place gravel or rounded stones on top of this if required. You can now fill the pond carefully with water.

Clay is different from other types of pond linings in that it is not crucial to get the edge level; any clay not covered by water will soon become colonized by waterside plants, or you can introduce your own varieties.

Bentonite clay can also be bought in blocks which should be laid tightly packed like brick paving.

Powdered clay can be purchased in bags. Mix this with water and spread it in a thick layer, keeping it wet by laying wet cloth over the parts you have finished. When the clay is in place, wet it and trample it thoroughly – a job most children are happy to help with. This forms a continuous layer which is waterproof as long as it is kept wet. Fill the pond immediately.

Bentonite is not readily available in water garden centres. You could try builders' merchants, or a water control company such as Rawell.

can be straight and formal like those in old Persian courtyards, or winding and informal, and as wide or narrow as you like, according to the style and size of your garden.

Concrete is probably the best material for making a canal because it is not restricted to shape, being able to mould around curves and corners. Clay, which is used for full-size canals, is another possibility. Flexible liner, which can be bought off a roll, is fine for a straight canal but would be difficult to curve around anything but the gentlest bend. A waterproof seal can be made by gluing two pieces of liner together, but it could be difficult to make the seal completely watertight.

In smaller gardens, summer houses and outdoor dining areas could be partly or totally surrounded by a moat, perhaps with a bridge or stepping stones across it, and mini-moats could be made along part of a garden boundary.

FLOWING WATER

Streams, waterfalls and fountains add interest to a water feature as well as oxygenating the water. A stream can be a habitat in itself as long as it does not flow faster than about 2m (6½ft) per second. If it is much faster than this, plants cannot root on the bottom, and floating plants and animals will be carried away.

A number of water plants will grow in moderately flowing water. These include watercress, starwort and common water crowfoot. Water lilies and most of the other more ornate aquatic plants do not like continually flowing water.

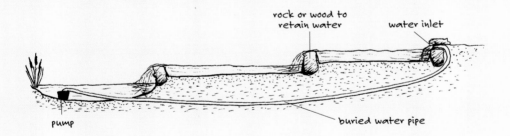

rock or wood to retain water

water inlet

pump

buried water pipe

Make a stream in sections so that the water doesn't run dry when the power is off

Unless you are lucky enough to have a natural stream in your garden you will need a pump that is sufficiently powerful to circulate the water through a piece of tubing from the lowest to the highest point. This is best installed by a professional electrician. The stream bed itself can be made of concrete, or pre-formed plastic or fibreglass sections. To avoid the stream running dry when the power is off, it should be made in sections which will hold water when the flow ceases.

See Tables 3.2–3.5
Pages 80-3

See Table 3.2
Page 80

WATER PLANTS

There is a wide choice of native plants suitable for a pond or stream, though some are too large and vigorous for a small water feature; yellow flag iris and the native water lilies, for example, are best avoided or they will take over in no time. A selection of smaller and less vigorous water plants is given in Tables 3.2–3.5.

For a good balance, select plants with different growth habits. Submerged oxygenators help keep the water aerated and fresh and support a variety of small creatures, including water snails. Avoid the commonly grown Canadian pondweed (*Elodea canadensis*): it spreads

PLANTING WATER PLANTS

Plants can be introduced into a pond or stream at any time during the growing season, although spring planting gives you longer to enjoy the plants during their first year's growth.

Oxygenating plants are often sold in bundles wrapped with a metal strip to weight them down. Simply drop these into the water and they will sink and root into the soil at the bottom of the pond. I recommend one bunch per 2m² (20ft²), though these plants will eventually spread.

Other aquatic plants can be planted directly into the bottom soil, but it is more convenient, and will also help to keep them under control, to plant them in perforated plastic containers; these can be bought from garden centres. Many plants come in pots and can be placed directly into the water.

To pot up a water plant, line the container with a piece of hessian to hold in the soil. Use garden soil or composted turf if available, otherwise buy a special compost for aquatic plants. Avoid soil or compost that is rich in organic matter; when this decays it will encourage the microscopic algae which discolour water (see page 77).

It is often recommended that water lilies and other bottom-rooted plants with floating leaves be introduced gradually to deeper water, to allow their stems time to grow to the required length. In my experience this is unnecessary; I have always just dropped them into the deepest part of a pool, and after a few days the leaves break the surface and the plant thrives.

Plants with floating leaves, like this water hawthorn (aponogeton), provide shelter for aquatic wildlife

so quickly you will be constantly pulling it out by the handful during the growing season. Native oxygenators like starwort and millfoil are slower growing and far more suitable. Some of the varieties in Table 3.2 have flowers on or above the water surface.

Plants with floating leaves shade the water from the sun, and this helps to keep down the algal growth that can colonize still water. Their leaves are strong enough to support insects and small birds which come to drink, and may provide stepping stones for frogs.

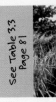

See Table 3.3
Page 81

Most of these plants are bottom rooted, but some are free floating. Bottom rooted plants with floating leaves, such as water lilies, tend to be long lived and, of course, to stay where they are. As they can spread, they need pulling out and dividing every few years. Some bottom rooters also have submerged leaves which oxygenate the water, for example, water crowfoot. Free-floating plants, such as frogbit, are easier to control but as they drift around, they may not stay where you want them; they are good for small ponds.

Marginal plants grow in the shallows at the water's edge. There is a great choice, depending on depth and size. A lush planting of marginals provides cover for amphibians and other creatures. Dragonflies lay their eggs on the stems of taller species, and their larvae climb from the water onto stems before hatching into adults.

Many water plants have colourful flowers; flying insects are attracted to these, and birds eat the seeds of some varieties.

See Table 3.4
Page 82

A broad-bodied, brown dragonfly laying its eggs among pool-side plants

BOG GARDENS

Many native plants like to grow in wet soil without actually standing in water. An area of marshy ground next to a pool or stream will support these and make an attractive transition between water and land. Even if you do not have a water feature it is worth making a small bog garden to support some of these varieties.

As with a pond, a garden marsh looks more natural in a low-lying part of the garden, and for the same reasons it should be in a sheltered, yet light and sunny spot, away from overhanging trees.

If your ground is naturally boggy, you may need to do nothing more than plant it up with suitable varieties; if not, you will need to use a pond liner to keep the soil wet.

There is a large choice of beautiful native plants that are suitable for a bog garden. A number of pond marginals also grow in damp soil (see Table 3.4), others prefer soil that is not saturated (see Table 3.5). Many marsh plants are annuals and biennials whose seeds germinate easily in wet soil. Some of the perennials are rather vigorous, and confining them to a bog garden will help dissuade them from spreading into the rest of the garden. Nevertheless, some underground roots or stems may escape; the iris I planted as a marginal some years ago has spread into the dry, sandy surroundings, no doubt still attached to the parent by rhizomes so it can get sufficient water.

Umbellifers, like this rare wild parsnip, grow well in wet meadows and marshes

See Table 3.5
Page 83

MAKING A BOG GARDEN

A bog garden next to water is easily made from flexible pond liner. The cheapest is polythene (1000 gauge), and being covered by soil, it is hidden from the sun's ultraviolet rays which make exposed polythene brittle. Alternatively, use a continuous piece of butyl or other good-quality liner for both pond and bog; this will allow the pond water to overflow into the bog.

The hole should have sloping sides, and be at least 30cm (12in) deep in the centre to reduce the risk of the marsh drying out in hot weather. The sloping sides will allow the ice to slip up and out of the hole, should the bog freeze, and thus help prevent damage to the lining from an expanding mass of ice. They will also provide different rooting depths in the bog to accommodate plants of different sizes. A stand-alone marsh or bog garden should be made in the same way as a pool-side marsh.

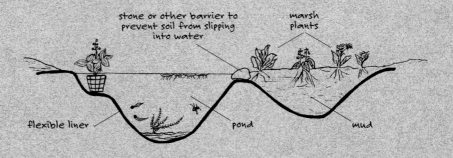

A bog garden next to an informal pond, made with a continuous piece of liner

When the liner is in place, fill it with garden soil. If the bog is continuous with the pool, place a barrier between the two to stop the marsh soil slipping into the water. This could be a row of smooth stones, for example, or a thick piece of old wood.

Concrete and clay ponds can be constructed similarly, with an adjoining bog garden lined with the same material.

In dry weather a bog habitat may need topping up, preferably with rainwater to avoid contamination from dissolved minerals in tap water.

Although marsh plants need permanently damp soil, most are unhappy if it becomes stagnant and airless. If waterlogging becomes a problem in a stand-alone marsh, pierce the liner at intervals with a garden fork to allow excess water to drain away. This cannot be done with a bog connected to a pool, for obvious reasons.

The best time to plant up a bog habitat is from April until early May, but container-grown plants can be added at any time.

Annuals and biennials can be grown from seeds and sown directly into the pond soil or, preferably, into small pots to give them a good start. Of course, seedlings and young plants must never be allowed to dry out.

An attractive planting scheme is to set plants in groups of each variety but allow them to intermingle.

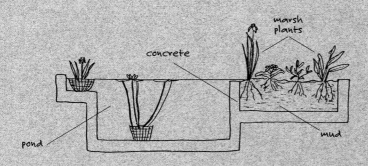

A bog garden built into the side of a formal concrete pond

MAINTENANCE AND PROBLEM SOLVING

Garden wetland habitats need very little maintenance and tend to look after themselves; in fact, it is best not to disturb them too much. Wildlife ponds should not be cleaned out too often because the detritus on the bottom provides food for scavengers and decomposers, so is vital for establishing a balanced ecology.

One 'problem' is that aquatic plants can grow too well, with vigorous varieties tending to take over. Excess oxygenators can be removed, but should be left next to the pond for a day or so to allow any pond creatures on them to return to the water.

A pair of mating blue damselflies on a pool-side plant

Overgrown marginals and marsh plants can be removed, split and replanted, using the younger portions round the edges of old clusters. This is best done in late spring or summer, when plants are growing strongly and after frogspawn and other eggs have hatched. Again, leave the unused bits next to the water: they will almost certainly contain small creatures which can return to their home.

Herbaceous perennial marginals and bog plants can be cut back in autumn to prevent their dead leaves from decaying and souring the water or marsh, although it is worth leaving the seed heads for feeding winter birds.

Pond and stream margins and marshes need to be weeded occasionally to keep unwanted invaders at bay, but fine grasses and other small colonizers can be kept as they look natural in a wildlife habitat and increase the biodiversity. Often a coating of lush moss will appear among the taller plants, and certain birds, among them robins, tits and greenfinches, will pull this off in chunks to line their nests.

Still water may turn green, red or even orange during the growing season in the first two or three years. This is due to coloured, microscopic algae which proliferate in a new pond, especially if it has been filled with tap water. For this reason, ponds should be topped up with rainwater, when necessary, as it contains no nutrients. The algae population will decrease as nutrients are used up. They will also be eaten by water fleas and other tiny herbivores, which will eventually increase in number and keep the algae under control.

A fine specimen of a marsh dragonfly

Dense waterside planting encourages shy creatures to visit your pond

Coloured water looks all right in an informal, wildlife pond, but if you really don't like it you can buy small pads of barley straw, sold in garden centres, to combat aquatic algae. These work by encouraging bacteria which attack the algae. After the first few years, when the pond ecology has become balanced, the water will remain clearer.

The same is true of blanket weed, that thick, matted algae which floats on pond surfaces. You can easily scoop it out, but eventually it will be kept under control by pond snails and other creatures. After a couple of years our small wildlife pool had no blanket weed and the water ceased to look like pea soup in summer. We are forever removing blanket weed from the goldfish pond, however: the fish eat the water fleas and shrimps which help to keep it down.

WETLAND WILDLIFE

Many animals live their whole life in water. Insects soon colonize a new pool, with water boatmen, whirligigs, diving beetles and pond skaters among the first to fly in. It is interesting to study them more closely. Pond skaters seem quite territorial, fighting briefly when they meet and pouncing upon unfortunate flies that fall in. Other carnivores include great diving beetles, huge insects which can startle when they suddenly appear at the surface to collect air, and water spiders which spin balloon-shaped webs underwater for catching prey. Dragonflies, mayflies, gnats and mosquitoes all lay their eggs in the water or on water plants, and their larvae are aqautic, in some cases spending several years under water before emerging as adults. Dragonfly larvae are fierce predators, feeding on tadpoles and aquatic insects, while the flat mayfly larvae lurk under pebbles, eating plankton and algae.

Frogs and newts soon arrive in garden ponds. With the loss of country ponds, frogs quickly spawn in a new home, but if this doesn't happen, introduce a small amount of spawn from an established pool. Newts' and toads' eggs are less visible: newts stick their eggs individually to underwater leaves, while double-stranded toad spawn sinks and becomes entangled with pondweed.

A little mud, water and weed from a local, established pond will introduce many interesting creatures. Tiny crustaceans, such as water fleas and fairy shrimps, help clear the water of algae, and detritus-eating caddis fly larvae build cases of silk, stones, shells and weeds for camouflage and protection. Others which might arrive in this way are snails, flatworms, leeches, hydrae, sponges and mites. If water snails are absent, introduce some: they are important scavengers of vegetable waste and multiply quickly, laying eggs in blocks of jelly on the leaves of water plants. Micro-scopic algae, diatoms, protozoa, rotifers and other microbes also inhabit pond water.

Pond and stream margins and bogs are also important for wildlife. Adult frogs, toads and newts hide in long, damp vegetation, coming out at night to eat garden slugs. Several bird species use mud; song thrushes, which feed on snails, line their grassy nests with mud, while house martins and swallows make their nests almost entirely from mud or clay, gathering it from marshy ground and ponds. It takes house martins about two weeks – and over 2,500 beaks full of mud – to make a nest, which they line with feathers, grass and straw. In a dry spell they delay making nests for weeks, and may fly long distances to get mud. At such times, a saucer of soil and water may help them. Blackbirds use mud to glue and line their nests. In spring, blackbirds are busy taking mud from my pond margins, leaving little hollows behind which fill with water.

TABLE 3.1

CHOOSING A POND LINER

Lining Material	Advantages	Disadvantages
Black polythene	Cheap, flexible	Deteriorates if exposed to sun's UV rays
Butyl rubber	Flexible, long lasting	More expensive than polythene
Pre-formed rigid plastic or fibreglass	Easy to install, long lasting	Limited shapes and sizes, may have steep sides
Reinforced concrete	Cheap, strong under pressure, any shape	Cracks under tension, toxic chemicals leach into water at first
Puddled clay	Cheap, any shape	Must be kept wet to avoid cracking

TABLE 3.2

SUBMERGED OXYGENATING PLANTS

Plant	Remarks
Curly pondweed *Potamogeton crispus*	Curly leaves. Flowers just above water surface
Hornwort *Ceratophyllum demersum*	Brittle, branched stems
Spiked water milfoil *Myriophyllum spicatum*	Feathery leaves. Insignificant flowers above the surface
Watercress *Rorippa nasturtium-aquaticum*	Edible, dark green or bronze-green leaves. Prefers flowing water
Water starwort *Callitriche stagnalis*	Pale green delicate-looking plant which can cope with occasional drying out. Grows in still or flowing water
Water violet *Hottonia palustris*	Finely divided yellow-green leaves. Pale lilac flower spikes above the water in May and June

Water violet flowers

TABLE 3.3

AQUATIC PLANTS WITH FLOATING LEAVES

Plant	Remarks
Amphibious bistort *Polygonum amphibium*	Oval leaves. Pink, cylindrical flower heads stand above the water in late summer. Snails stick their eggs to the underside of the leaves

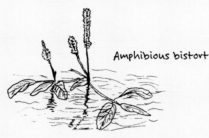

Amphibious bistort

Plant	Remarks
Broad-leaved pondweed *Potamogeton natans*	Dark green, oval leaves. Insignificant flowers
Frogbit *Hydrocharis morsus-ranae*	Floating plant with rounded leaves. Dainty, three-petalled white flowers above the water in spring. It forms buds which sink in autumn, then rise to the surface in spring
Water crowfoot *Ranunculus aquatilis*	White-flowered buttercup which grows in still and running water. Indented floating leaves and finely divided submerged leaves. Prefers shallow water, tolerates occasional drying out
Water fringe *Nymphoides peltata*	Similar to water lilies in habit. Circular leaves. Three-petalled yellow flowers just above the water from May to August
Water lilies *Nymphaea* spp.	Small varieties for shallow ponds include *N. odorata* 'Turicensis', with scented pale pink flowers, and the miniature *N. pygmaea helvola*, with yellow flowers and olive leaves speckled with red

Water crowfoot

TABLE 3.4

PLANTS FOR POND MARGINS

Plant	Remarks
Bog bean *Menyanthes trifoliata*	Delicate white or pink flowers from May to July. Blue-green leaves resembling those of broad beans
Brooklime *Veronica beccabunga*	Bright blue flowers. Fleshy leaves
Burr reed *Sparganium erectum*	Globular flowers and spiky round fruits. Strap-like leaves. Birds eat the seeds
Dwarf reed mace *Typha minima*	A miniature bulrush, 30cm (12in) high. Tiny, brownish, poker-head flowers in June and July. Strap-like leaves. Sparrows eat the ripe seeds
Flowering rush *Butomus umbellatus*	Pink-mauve flower clusters; slender green leaves
Lesser spearwort *Ranunculus flammula*	Bright yellow buttercup flowers. Prefers shallow water
Marsh marigold *Caltha palustris*	Golden, cup-shaped flowers in early spring which are attractive to insects, including butterflies, just out of their hibernation. Prefers shallow water
Water forget-me-not *Myosotis palustris*	Small, pale blue flowers in May and June. Prefers shallow water, still or flowing. Self seeds readily. 'Semperflorens' is a more compact variety
Water mint *Mentha aquatica*	Scented leaves. Pink flower clusters in late summer, attractive to butterflies and bees
Water plantain *Alisma graminium,* *A. lanceolatum*	Candelabra sprays of mauve-pink flowers. Prefers shallow water. Self seeds readily

Water mint

Marsh marigold

TABLE 3.5

MARSH PLANTS

Plant	Remarks
Creeping jenny *Lysimachia nummularia*	Low, spreading stems with bright yellow flowers
Hemp agrimony *Eupatorium cannabinum*	Perennial with flat heads of dusty pink flowers, followed by fluffy seed heads. Attracts bees and butterflies
Fleabane *Pulicaria dysenterica*	Creeping perennial with yellow daisy-like flowers in late summer which attract many insects
Hairy willowherb *Epilobium hirsutum*	Deep pink flowers popular with bees. Hairy stems and foliage. Self seeds readily
Hemp agrimony *Eupatorium cannabinum*	Flat, loose heads of pink flowers, from July to October, attract butterflies and other insects
Marsh cinquefoil *Potentilla palustris*	Creeping perennial with red, star-like flowers and purple fruits which resemble strawberries
Marsh woundwort *Stachys palustris*	Pale purple flowers from July onwards, attractive to bees
Meadowsweet *Filipendula ulmaria*	Fragrant, creamy flower heads in July
Purple loosestrife *Lythrum salicaria*	Spectacular magenta flower spikes attract butterflies in August
Ragged robin *Lychnis flos-cuculi*	Rare annual with raggy pink flowers in June which attract butterflies and bumblebees. Its delicate clove scent attracts night moths
Salad burnet *Sanguisorba minor*	Red-purple flowers and edible leaves
Saw-wort *Serratula tinctoria*	A relative of knapweeds, with red-purple flower heads. Prefers limy soil
Yellow loosestrife *Lysimachia vulgaris*	Perennial, unrelated to purple loosestrife. Its yellow spires are visited almost exclusively by one type of bee. Its leaves are the only food of a rare weevil

Ragged robin

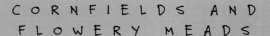

4

CORNFIELDS AND
FLOWERY MEADS

Grassland habitats

Apart from mountain meadows and sheep-cropped
pastures above the tree line, most British grasslands are
not strictly natural. If left unmanaged, grassland would
revert to woodland within a few decades.

GRASSLAND HISTORY

Originally forest, much of what is now grassland in Britain was systematically cleared for farming by our ancestors. Centuries of traditional farming practices, using crop rotation, livestock grazing and fertilization, have led to the development of rich meadow, cornfield and heath communities. Many of the plants and animals that inhabit these sites were once, before mankind's intervention, rare, transient species visiting forest clearings where trees had fallen, animal tracks, or shifting stream banks.

Flowery meadows are now rare in the countryside

It is ironic, therefore, that mankind's activities since the mid-1900s have damaged and destroyed the same grasslands that he helped to create. Modern agricultural methods, including crop monoculture, the widespread use of herbicides and other chemicals, and the decline of common grazing land, together with land clearance for roads and buildings, have resulted in the loss of most of Britain's unimproved pasture, along with its wildflowers and their dependent insects. Flowers such as corncockle, cornflower, cowslip and many orchids are now rare or extinct in the wild. As a result, butterflies such as the common blue and meadow brown are also in decline, and even grasshoppers are threatened in many regions.

MEDIEVAL TURF BENCHES

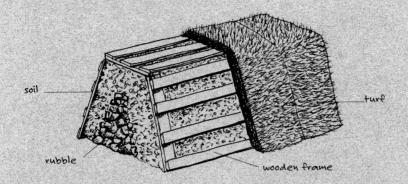

soil — rubble — wooden frame — turf

The turf bench was a favourite piece of medieval garden furniture

These benches were often built against walls or encircling large trees. Sometimes they were sheltered by pergolas covered with vines and other climbers. A raised bank of earth, supported by boards, bricks or wattle (woven branches), was covered with grass and small flowering plants.

A painting by the Meister des Marienlebens, dated around 1470, depicts the Madonna and Child seated on turf benches in a beautiful garden. The benches are planted with madonna lilies and other flowers, while the mead is colourful with daisies, dandelions and strawberries. The benches' occupants are protected from the sun by arching pergolas entwined with vines and white double roses.

A turf bench would make an unusual garden feature. As well as being a seat, it would double as a three-dimensional meadow habitat. It would look best in a sheltered, informal part of the garden, particularly if wildflowers were allowed to grow in the surrounding lawn.

To make a turf bench, first construct the sides from wooden boards or open brickwork. Fill the centre with rubble, for bulk, then soil, and compact well. Top with a board or planks to provide support, then cover with a fine grass turf and plant small meadow flowers in holes cut into the grass. Keep well watered and do not sit on it for a few weeks, until the plants are established.

Small flowers you could try include violets, primroses, lesser periwinkle, clover, daisies, buttercups, and wild strawberries.

GRASSLAND WILDLIFE

A holly blue butterfly alighting on a daisy in order to feed on its nectar

The most evident wildlife creatures of a flowering meadow are the many varieties of butterfly which feed on the nectar. If you are lucky enough to live near an area of sympathetically managed grassland, your meadow may even be visited by now-rare varieties like the meadow brown, small heath, common blue and green hairstreak. It's not just the adult insects that need open grassland; some butterflies and moths lay their eggs on grass stems so the larvae can feed there. You may find pupae suspended on the grass.

Spider gossamer coating long grass on a summer's day

Hedgehogs are useful predators of slugs and snails

Bees, hoverflies and various other flying insects also visit grassland wildflowers for nectar and pollen. Heard more often than seen, grasshoppers and crickets are now endangered in parts of Britain. There are several species, the most common of which is the meadow grasshopper. Flightless, with vestigial wings, grasshoppers are fussy eaters, feeding mainly on grass and a few other plants. They are known for their distinctive sound which is made by their legs moving up and down, rubbing against a hardened patch on their front wings.

Multitudes of shy creatures inhabit long grass. Look closely and you should see that your meadow is crawling with insects and spiders. On a damp day, spiders' webs become visible, coating the grass to catch anything that passes.

Grassland invertebrates attract larger carnivores like hedgehogs, shrews and birds. Long grass also provides damp cover for frogs and other amphibians.

The immaculate lawn, dutifully mown twice a week and not a weed in sight, is a relatively recent garden feature. In medieval Europe, lawns were allowed to grow long during spring and early summer and were deliberately planted with flowers to make flowery meads. These were not only ornamental but were also used for recreational purposes. In *The Franklin's Tale*, Chaucer describes a mead, planted with sweet williams, primroses, violets and daisies, used as a dance floor. The inhabitants also told stories and played games, including chess, on their meads.

Meadow brown butterflies are now rare due to a loss of grasslands

Modern lawns are quite sterile in comparison. The advent of the mechanical lawn mower and weed-killing chemicals have made the plain, closely cropped lawn almost ubiquitous. Now, however, some brave gardeners are daring to let their grass grow. If recent trends continue, the flowery mead may become popular again.

TYPES OF GRASSLAND

Perhaps the most widespread grassland in Britain today is that found on the fertile loams and clays of central and south-east England. Much of this is farmed, grazed by animals or mown for hay. The soil is near neutral, and many plant species grow here. Most of the 'weeds' are deep-rooted, rosette or scrambling plants which can withstand grazing or cutting and compete well with the grasses. They include clovers, buttercups, plantain, thistles, lady's smock, meadowsweet, trefoils and vetches.

Large areas of southern England have shallow chalk soil which dries out quickly. The fine grasses which grow here make good grazing land. Flowers include yarrow, thistles, trefoil, rock rose, knapweed, hawkweed, restharrow, plantain, scabious, dandelion and wild thyme. Chalk grassland is known for the many varieties of butterflies attracted to its wildflowers.

A similar grassland type, also alkaline and found in many hilly regions, grows in limestone soil. This too is fast draining. Suitable flowers include harebell, salad burnet, and most of those that grow well on chalk.

Tufted vetch may be found in summer meadows with poor soil

A very different type of grassland, found in other hilly areas, is known as siliceous grassland. The soil here is poor, thin and acidic, with most of the nutrients washed out by high rainfall. Sheep grazing is common in these parts. Heathers are dominant in places, along with crowberry, bog asphodel and other suitable wildflowers, including bilberry, cowberry, cross-leaved heath, harebell, sedges and rushes.

Some of these permanent grassland types are ancient and have developed a very rich flora over many centuries. Arable farming, on the other hand, ploughs up the ground annually and hence, at least until modern herbicides came into widespread use, encouraged the growth of quick-growing annuals, such as poppies, whose seeds germinate well on disturbed ground.

These are the main grasslands found in Britain today, but there are many subdivisions of these, and other types, depending on soil, climate and history. For example, some areas near the coast will have sandy soil which has its own ecology, including plants adapted to sand dunes, mud flats and beaches, while other areas may be reclaimed from marshes and have damp peat or silt soil. To discover which grassland wildflowers will grow well in your garden, make a note of the dominant varieties in nearby fields, verges or wasteland.

GARDEN GRASSLAND HABITATS

It is encouraging to see that keepers of many large public gardens, including the botanical gardens at Kew and Cambridge and certain National Trust properties, are leaving large areas of lawn uncut during spring and early summer. The lacy grass flowers, interspersed with oxeye daisies, buttercups, cow parsley and orchids, are far more interesting than the closely mown areas.

Toadflax will readily colonize a garden grassland habitat

Small gardens too can play their part in the revival of the flowery mead. My own spring meadow occupies an area of just 1m (3ft) in diameter in a sheltered corner of the lawn and I cut the surrounding grass normally. The meadow area, containing cowslips, forget-me-nots, buttercups and daisies, looks good in its setting, and more wildflower varieties are moving in each year.

There are several types of grassland habitat and all of them, surprisingly for some examples, can be introduced into a garden in miniature. You will have most success if you select grass and flower varieties which suit the conditions in your region.

Oxeye daisies and other flowers can be grown in a lawn to make a flowery meadow

CORNFIELDS

Unlike most other grassland habitats, a cornfield has annual wildflowers only temporarily, although most of these self seed reliably and may well return the following year. Some cornfield weeds are common on waste ground and in gardens, especially when the soil is disturbed or first cultivated. When buried, their seeds can lie dormant for many years; tilling the soil exposes the seeds to light, which causes germination. The summer after I dug up half of our back lawn, the resulting flower bed was full of poppies whose seeds had been buried for decades. Other cornfield annuals, for example the beautiful corncockle, have become rare since agricultural herbicide use increased.

See Table 4.1 Page 105

Annual wildflowers originally grew in temporarily disturbed ground such as shingle and collapsed river banks. When farming began, these annuals thrived and multiplied in the ploughed fields, in competition with crops. Apparently, medieval bread had an interesting effect if the corn had become contaminated with opium-containing poppy seed heads.

Many cornfield annuals have brightly coloured flowers and make an attractive display during summer. Some of them are already grown in gardens as ornamental flowers, while others are usually treated as weeds. They look splendid grown as part of a mixed flower bed and are popular with butterflies, bees and other insects.

MEADOWS

Traditional farming methods encouraged wildflowers to grow in meadows. The species which flourished depended on the management regime and the time of harvest as well as the soil, climate and other conditions. In general, meadows

Poppies are beautiful cornfield annuals

MAKING A CORNFIELD HABITAT

Part of a flowerbed can be set aside for a cornfield; it should be in an open, sunny spot. Dig the area over and remove any perennial weeds, then leave for a week or two and hoe off any seedlings which appear.

Mixtures of cornfield annual seeds can be purchased, and this is the cheapest means of planting up a small area, but individual varieties are available if preferred. Alternatively, you can gather seeds from common annuals growing wild.

In spring or autumn, scatter the seeds thinly and rake them into the surface. Fertilizer is not required; in fact, you will get better results in poor soil. Remove any obvious perennial weed seedlings, such as nettles or thistles, but don't worry about grass or small annual weeds as they will enhance the overall effect. The seeds germinate very easily in spring, and the following summer you will be rewarded with a colourful patch of flowers, popular with bees, hoverflies, butterflies and moths.

To re-create the cornfield the following year, allow the plants to seed, clear the ground in autumn or spring, then rake the soil to disturb it. This exposes more seeds to light and loosens the soil, so helping germination.

would be cut to produce a commercial hay crop some time during mid- or late summer, then grazed by livestock over autumn and winter. This grazing prevented coarse grasses and vigorous perennials, like thistles, nettles and docks, from suffocating the meadow flowers, and the animals' hooves churned up the soil surface which helped the flower seeds reach soil where they could germinate.

Although farming practices have changed, many nature reserves and conservation sites contain flower meadows; some are harvested commercially, others are grown solely for their wildlife value. Larger sites may be grazed by sheep or cattle for part of the year; smaller areas, including roadside verges, are cut manually.

Normal garden mowing, where the grass is cut low and often, is intended to encourage a dense grass carpet at the expense of wildflowers. Some lawn 'weeds', however, have adapted to this regime, forming low mats or rosettes; these include daisies, dandelions, creeping speedwell, white clover, plantain, cat's-ear and selfheal. Many gardeners kill these off with selective weedkiller or, if they are using organic methods, dig them out and re-seed with grass.

Bladder campion is a common plant of road verges and summer meadows

Admittedly, a well-tended lawn looks splendid, but so does a patch of grass where daisies, clover and speedwell are allowed to flower. Whatever your taste in lawns, a small patch left to flower is an attractive feature, especially if the surrounding lawn is kept neat. Many wildflowers, like cowslip and scabious, grow and look better in grass than in flowerbeds. A circle or irregular area of approximately 1m² (10ft²) is a suitable size for a small garden although, of course, a larger area can be used.

Several factors affect which plant varieties will grow well in your garden meadow. Your soil type is important, especially if it has an unusually high or low pH; chalk grasslands support very different flora from peaty heaths. The climate, and whether your ground is well drained or soggy, shaded or sunny, are all things to be considered when deciding what to grow. As with all gardening, though, it is worth experimenting – you could be pleasantly surprised with the results.

There are two ways of making a permanent meadow. The easiest is to stop mowing a piece of the lawn for part of the year and allow what wildflowers appear to grow. Alternatively, a new meadow can be sown from scratch. Since meadow flowers bloom during different

See Table 4.2
Page 106

HARVESTING A GARDEN MEADOW

A meadow must be harvested at least once a year to remove the hay, reduce fertility, and prevent grass and vigorous perennials from swamping the wildflowers.

Commercial hay meadows, nature reserves, commons and large-scale ornamental meadows are generally cut annually, perhaps with sheep or other livestock grazing for part of the year. A small garden habitat, on the other hand, needs to look relatively neat, so a spring or summer meadow regime is best.

Choose a dry spell for cutting the hay. A strimmer is ideal for this task, or you could practise your skill with a scythe. For very small meadows, a pair of shears will do the job. The hay should be left for a few days to dry and then tossed to shake out the ripe seeds.

The medievals used their fragrant hay for mattresses and soft furnishings; today it makes a useful addition to the compost heap or mulch around young trees and shrubs.

Spring meadow

To encourage bulbs and other spring flowers, harvest the meadow in July and mow normally for the rest of the year. This frees the lawn for use over the summer and is the best type of meadow in a small garden.

Summer meadow

To encourage summer flowers, mow as normal until June, then leave until mid-September before harvesting and mowing normally for the rest of the year. Avoid walking on a summer meadow whenever possible.

seasons, some in spring and others in summer, what you grow will also depend on your mowing regime and what you use the lawn for.

Spring meadows

Spring meadows are the most popular type of grassland habitat in gardens, not least because they are mown from July onwards, in time for summer and the barbecue season. In fact, walking on a mown spring meadow actually helps the flowers to spread, in the same way that grazing animals aided the old hay meadows. Also, spring meadow flowers tend to be small and non-vigorous, ideal for a small habitat. Some wildflowers will colonize naturally, and others are easy to introduce.

See Table 4.3
Page 107

SOWING A NEW MEADOW

The quickest way of creating a meadow habitat is to sow a suitable mixture of grass and wildflower seeds. The site can be in sun or part shade and on any soil, from well drained to boggy. Different plants will thrive in different conditions, the only rule is that soil should be of low fertility so that it favours a range of meadow flowers over grasses. If your intended site is fertile, remove the turf or topsoil and replace it with subsoil or poor soil mixed with sharp sand. Alternatively, if you are not in a hurry, cultivate the site for a year or two without adding fertilizer.

Prepare the site as for sowing a normal lawn. Dig it over, removing large stones and perennial weed roots, then rake the surface to a fine tilth. It is a good idea at this stage to leave it for two or three weeks to allow weed seeds to germinate. These can then be hoed off and any missed bits of perennials which have sprouted can be pulled up. Repeat this process after another interval if required.

For a small area it is cheapest to use a meadow seed mixture, available from specialist nurseries, mail-order companies and some garden centres in packets or by weight. Some merchants supply special mixes for different mowing regimes and growing conditions. Meadow seed mixtures generally consist of around 80% fine grasses, such as fescues and bents, with 20% mixed wildflowers. You could add a selection of cornfield annual seeds for colour during the first growing season.

Early autumn and mid spring are the best times to sow; the soil should be damp. Give the ground a final rake, then firm it. A garden roller is useful for larger areas, but medium to small areas are best firmed by close treading over the whole area. Meadow seed should be sown more sparsely than normal lawn seed – 2–3g (one level tsp) per m² (1y²) or according to the instructions on the packet. It will help you spread the seed more evenly if you first mix it with silver sand, as this makes it obvious where it has already been sown. Broadcast first in one direction, then the other, then rake lightly to cover the seeds. To keep off birds and cats, lay twiggy prunings on the seed bed until the grass has sprouted. If it doesn't rain during the first few weeks after sowing, water thoroughly with a fine spray.

In the first year, keep the meadow mown to 5–7.5cm (2–3in): this will encourage the grasses to spread and cover the ground. Rake off the clippings carefully to keep fertility low. If you've included cornfield annuals, only mow from late summer, after the annuals have flowered. Begin your mowing regime from the second year, to encourage the flowers to bloom and spread. When the meadow is established, you can add more varieties by planting pot-grown wildflowers amongst the grass.

CONVERTING PART OF A LAWN INTO A MEADOW

In an established garden, the easiest way to make a meadow is to leave a section of the lawn, especially if it is poor and weedy, uncut for part of the year. The most colourful meadows grow on poor soil. They should never be fed and, when cut, the clippings must always be removed to reduce soil fertility.

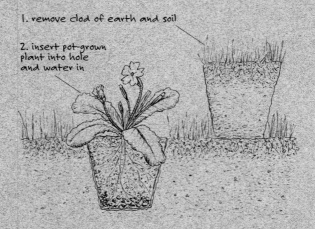

1. remove clod of earth and soil

2. insert pot-grown plant into hole and water in

Planting a pot-grown plant into a meadow

There may already be some wildflowers present, and others will arrive naturally. These include common lawn 'weeds' like buttercups, speedwell and yarrow which are usually discouraged. Rarer varieties can be introduced as pot-grown plants, either purchased or from seeds sown thinly in small pots. This is more successful than direct sowing. Try collecting a few seeds from common flowers in verges. Sow them as fresh as possible and leave the pots outdoors. The seeds may not germinate until the following spring. Pot the seedlings separately. When the young plants are large enough, dig holes in the turf, insert the plants and water well.

In a meadow made from an established lawn, it may take a few years for the flowers to grow better than the grasses. One problem, particularly with summer meadows, is that coarse, vigorous grasses like rye, included in lawns because they are hard-wearing, tend to take over at first. If large clumps form, dig them out and re-seed with finer varieties or replace with meadow wildflowers.

MEADOW BULBS

1. remove layer of turf

2. plant bulbs in a group

3. replace turf

Plant bulbs randomly in groups, under turf, in a spring meadow

Spring meadows in particular are ideal for growing some of Britain's native and naturalized bulb and corm flowers. There is a surprising selection (see Table 4.4). Some of these flowers are now very rare in the wild, although they are commonly grown in gardens and parks. Most flower in spring, so the grass should not be cut until the plants' leaves start to die back. This allows the bulbs to bulk up, ready to produce flowers the following year.

Meadow saffron (*Colchicum autumnale*) is an exception, flowering in autumn. This, and cultivated varieties, are often seen in parks, grouped under trees. Its long leaves appear in late spring, so saffron suits a spring meadow which should also be left uncut in autumn.

Bulbs and corms can be planted in autumn, in groups and drifts, before a new meadow is sown. For an established meadow, dig up pieces of turf, bury groups of bulbs at the required depth, then replace the turf.

Spring bulb flowers are important early nectar providers for insects, like bumblebees and butterflies, emerging from hibernation at this time.

Summer meadows

Summer meadows contain plants which flower from mid- to late summer. There is a huge choice. (Table 4.3 lists some of the smaller varieties – up to 60cm (24in) tall – suitable for a small meadow habitat.) If you can spare a patch of lawn for the required growing season – summer meadows should not be walked on when they are in active growth – a summer meadow is a beautiful garden feature.

See Table 4.4 Page 108

WASTELAND HABITATS

Places where conditions are too extreme for arable farming are known collectively as wastelands. These increasingly threatened regions include upland and lowland heath, grazing marshes, mud flats, sand and shingle near the coast, rocky and stony ground, swamps and fens (see Chapter 3).

Some grasses thrive in the harsh conditions that exist near the coast

Harebells are dainty plants for small garden meadows and heaths

Some of these habitats are now small and isolated. Soil is generally poor and the climate may be hostile, so plants found in these places have become adapted to the stressful conditions. It is possible to create small versions in gardens. Since there are so many types of wasteland habitats it is impossible to cover them all here, so we'll look at two examples: sand dune and acid heath.

Sand dune

Near the coast, the ground may be sandy or rocky and will not easily support a conventional meadow. Instead, you could grow some of the wildflowers which thrive on sand dunes, shingle and cliff tops. The land here is very well drained and tends to heat and cool quickly. The associated plants are very deep rooted – over 2m (6½ft) in some cases – in order to reach fresh water underground. Some have extensive root networks which stabilize sand dunes and shingle beaches, and hence help to protect the coastline from erosion. Their leaves are narrow, waxy or succulent, in order to slow water loss. Some species can survive being submerged by wind-blown sand and shingle.

See Table 4.5
Page 109

Sand dune habitats are not limited to coastal areas. Breckland in Norfolk, for example, contains large regions of sand over chalk bedrock, and many of the wildflowers found there also grow on sand dunes. In fact, a sand dune habitat can be grown in almost any garden; at the Stoke-on-Trent National Garden Festival in 1986, one of the demonstration gardens had a heap of sand in one corner planted up with sand dune grasses and wildflowers – an interesting and unusual feature.

Acid heath

See Table 4.6 Page 110

Heath grassland can be high or low lying, wet or dry and with sandy or peat soil. Each type has its own flora. In the wild, plants are often grazed by sheep and rabbits. This keeps the vegetation short and prevents gorse, broom and other scrub from invading.

Bracken is a big problem in large areas of heathland – it spreads vigorously and smothers small and delicate wildflowers. Once there, it is a constant battle to control it. Active clearing of bracken and scrub is carried out by volunteers in nature reserves and other conservation sites.

If your soil is acid, you could grow some of the beautiful heathers and other wildflowers of acid heathland, most of which are actually low-growing shrubs rather than herbaceous plants like other grassland wildflowers. The soil must be very infertile. To mimic grazing and prevent them from becoming tall and woody, trim the heather, grasses and other plants with shears or a strimmer after flowering.

GRASSES AND THEIR RELATIVES

See Table 4.7 Page 111

I have left the dominant grassland plants till last. It is easy to take grasses for granted, seeing them merely as forming green matrices for lawns, parks and playing fields, but there is an amazing variety of grasses, as becomes evident when a portion of lawn is left to grow to flowering size.

Grasses are very diverse plants. Because of this, there are varieties found in most habitats, including rocklands, woods, beaches and water. Most are perennials, though there are a few annuals. Their massed flowers are beautiful, giving summer meadows a purplish mistiness. It would be worth growing a grassland habitat for the grasses alone, even if no other wildflowers moved in.

Grass flowers come in many shapes and colours

Like any other type of plant, different grasses prefer different conditions. Fescue grasses like neutral to alkaline soil, for example, while bent grasses prefer it on the acid side. Grass seed mixes include common grasses that are not too fussy about where they grow. It is possible to buy mixes for unusual or extreme conditions, which is useful if you garden on very sandy, chalky or damp ground. Avoid those including coarse grasses such as rye and cocksfoot, which are too vigorous for small garden meadows.

field woodrush   common sedge   wall barley   common quaking grass

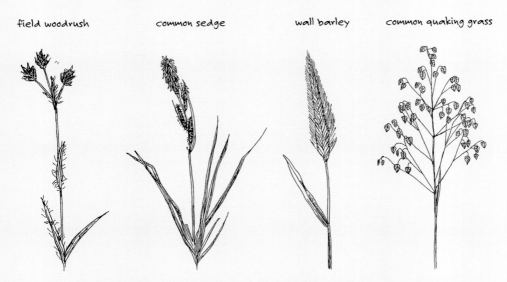

Grasses produce a variety of beautiful flower forms not normally appreciated in a garden

Grass flowers give summer meadows a purple tinge

Close relatives of grasses include sedges and rushes. Their leaves and flowers resemble those of grasses, but they need very infertile and usually damp ground to grow well. Some varieties have declined in numbers due to the drainage and fertilization of farmland.

Rushes and sedges form dense tussocks. Sedges have solid stems with triangular cross sections, distinguishing them from grasses, which have hollow, round flower stems. Rushes produce small, green, brown or yellow flowers. The related woodrushes have flat, hairy leaves and grow on drier ground than rushes. If you have very poor soil, particularly if it is wet, some of these plants may already be growing.

TABLE 4.1

CORNFIELD ANNUALS

Plant	Remarks
Chamomile *Matricaria chamomilla*	A common weed of sandy soils. White, daisy-like flower heads with yellow conical centres from May to August. Finely divided leaves. It has a distinctive aroma
Corncockle *Agrostemma githago*	Tall, with mauve-pink flowers from June to September. Fertilized by butterflies and moths. Extremely rare in the wild
Cornflower *Centaurea cyanus*	A popular garden flower but rare in the wild. Blue flower heads are the most common, although garden varieties are available in mauve, pink and white shades
Corn marigold *Chrysanthemum segetum*	Yellow flower heads similar to those of pot marigolds. Rare in the wild
Fumitory *Fumaria officinalis*	Loose spikes of small, pink flowers from May to October, visited by bees. Lacy, divided leaves
Heartsease *Viola tricolor*	This small pansy has flowers which vary in size and colour. It is popular with bees and butterflies
Mayweed *Matricaria inodora*	Very similar to corn chamomile in appearance, but scentless. Flowers from June to October
Poppy *Papaver rhoeas*	Bright red flowers from June to September, visited by bees and hoverflies. Its seeds can survive in soil for many years. Common on verges and wasteland
Red dead-nettle *Lamium purpureum*	Low growing, with square stems, purple-tinged leaves, and mauve-red flowers from April to October. Common throughout Britain
Scarlet pimpernel *Anagallis arvensis*	Low growing, with small, red flowers which close up in dull weather. Pink- and blue-flowered forms are sometimes found. Common in sandy soil

Heartsease

Poppy

TABLE 4.2

GRASSLAND BULBS AND CORMS

Plant	Remarks
Crocus *Crocus vernus*	Naturalized in parts of Britain. Mauve flowers in March. Provides pollen for bees. Grows in sun or partial shade, including under trees
Daffodil *Narcissus pseudonarcissus*	Smaller than most garden varieties. Pale yellow flowers in April. Grows in sun or partial shade, including under trees
Fritillary *Fritillaria meleagris*	Chequered pink-purple or white bell flowers. Butterflies feed on the nectar. Will spread in damp conditions
Grape hyacinth *Muscari neglectum*	Rare in the wild but common in gardens. Prefers sunny site and dry grassland. Deep blue or white flower heads. Important nectar plant for butterflies
Meadow saffron *Colchicum autumnale*	A rare native, often grown in parks. Pink, lilac or white flowers in autumn. Grows in well-drained soil in sun or partial shade, including under trees. Attracts bumblebees and butterflies
Snowflake *Leucojum vernum*	Similar to snowdrop, but larger and later flowering. Very rare wildflower. Likes moist soil

Daffodil

TABLE 4.3

SPRING MEADOW FLOWERS

Plant	Remarks
Bugle *Ajuga reptans*	Creeping perennial with mauve flower spikes. It will flourish in any conditions, including shade
Cowslip *Primula veris*	Pale yellow flower clusters over rosettes of wrinkled leaves. Self seeds readily. Important nectar source for early butterflies. Food plant for fritillary caterpillars
Creeping speedwell *Veronica filiformis*	Small, spreading plant with small, blue flowers, attractive to butterflies
Daisy *Bellis perennis*	Surely the most common wildflower. Forms spreading mats. White flowers, sometimes tinged pink, with yellow centres. Its seeds are dispersed by ants
Dandelion *Taraxacum officinale*	Its golden flowers are popular with many insects. Remove fading flowers to prevent prolific seeding, although bullfinches enjoy eating the seeds
Germander speedwell *Veronica chamaedrys*	Similar to creeping speedwell, but taller growing. Small, blue flowers from March to June
Lady's smock *Cardamine pratensis*	Pale mauve or pink flowers. Food plant for orange-tip butterfly caterpillars. Prefers damp conditions
Lesser stitchwort *Stellaria graminea*	Starry white flowers, popular with bees, butterflies and moths
Meadow saxifrage *Saxifraga granulata*	Delicate white flowers from April to June. Kidney-shaped, lobed leaves. Prefers neutral to alkaline, well-drained soil
Yellow rattle *Rhimnanthus minor*	Yellow-flowered annual, semi-parasitic on grasses. Its seeds rattle in their large seed pods

Dandelion

TABLE 4.4

SUMMER MEADOW FLOWERS

Plant	Remarks
Bladder campion *Silene vulgaris*	Shorter than the similar white campion. Visited by moths and bees
Devil's bit scabious *Succisa pratensis*	Smaller and darker blue flowers than those of the taller field scabious. Attracts butterflies. Food plant for caterpillars of the marsh fritillary butterfly
Field buttercup *Ranunculus acris*	Its golden flowers attract insects, including butterflies and day-flying moths. Wood pigeons eat its seeds
Kidney vetch *Anthyllis vulneraria*	Pea family member with yellow flower heads. Pollinated by bees. Hairy, compound leaves
Lady's bedstraw *Galium verum*	Clusters of small, scented, yellow flowers. Attracts butterflies, hawk moths and other flying insects. Food plant for several moth caterpillars
Hedgerow cranesbill *Geranium pyrenaicum*	Purple flowers. Its seeds, sometimes eaten by bullfinches, are hurled explosively from the dry fruits on hot days
Oxeye daisy *Chrysanthemum leucanthemum*	Large, white daisy flowers. Visited by many kinds of flying insects
Red clover *Trifolium pratense*	Globular, crimson flower heads and attractive trifoliate leaves
Sorrel *Rumex acetosa*	Red flower spikes. Bullfinches and goldfinches eat the seeds. Small copper butterflies lay eggs on the leaves
Silverweed *Potentilla anserina*	Buttercup-like flowers visited by insects. Serrated leaflets covered with silky hairs underneath. Spreads by runners. Prefers moist grassland
St John's Wort *Hypericum perforatum*	Bright yellow flowers, each with three bunches of large stamens. Likes chalky soil
Toadflax *Linaria vulgaris*	Yellow flowers like small snapdragons. Fertilized by bees. Narrow leaves
Yarrow *Achillea millefolium*	White or pale lilac, flat flower heads and finely divided leaves. Important nectar plant

Field buttercup

TABLE 4.5

SAND DUNE PLANTS

Plant	Remarks
Bird's-foot trefoil *Lotus corniculatus*	Also called bacon-and-eggs because its yellow flowers are streaked with red. Common on dry grassland throughout Britain, it thrives on sand and shingle along the coast
Centaury *Centaurium erythraea*	Annual with clusters of pink, or sometimes white, starry flowers
Dog violet *Viola canina*	Deep violet flowers from March to June. Dislikes limy soil. Its seeds are dispersed by ants
English stonecrop *Sedum anglicum*	Forms spreading mats of fleshy leaves which are blue-green tinged with red. Pale pink flowers and red fruits. Prefers acid soil, disliking chalk and lime
Horned poppy *Glaucium flavum*	Biennial or short-lived perennial which often flowers the first year from seed. Large yellow flowers from June to September, each lasting just one day. Long, narrow seed heads. Visited by bees and hoverflies for its pollen
Hottentot fig *Carpobrotus edulis*	A South African import, naturalized in Devon, Cornwall and the Scilly Isles. Similar to mesembryanthemum, with yellow or red daisy-like flowers. Hardy in mild coastal areas
Sea campion *Silene vulgaris* subsp. *maritima*	Close relative of bladder campion, with white flowers from July to September
Sea holly *Eryngium maritimum*	Prickly silver leaves and thistle-like, metallic-blue flowers. Attracts bees, butterflies and beetles for its nectar. Increasingly rare on sand dunes and shingle

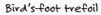

Bird's-foot trefoil

Sea campion

TABLE 4.6

ACID HEATH PLANTS

Plant	Remarks
Bilberry *Vaccinium myrtillus*	Also called whortleberry. A low-growing, deciduous shrub, abundant on some heaths. Small, rose-pink flowers, followed by edible, juicy, blue-black berries
Cowberry or mountain cranberry *Vaccinium vitis-idaea*	Prostrate evergreen shrub. White or pale pink flower racemes in May and June, followed by dark red berries which may last well into winter
Cross-leaved heather *Erica tetralix*	Small shrub, with drooping mauve flowers from July to September which provide nectar for bees. It grows in damp, acid soil
Crowberry *Empetrum nigrum*	Low, trailing shrub similar to heaths. Tiny, red-purple flowers in spring. Its black fruits are edible
Harebell *Campanula rotundifolia*	Blue bellflowers from July to September, pollinated by bees and visited by many flying insects
Heather or ling *Calluna vulgaris*	Common shrub of heath and moorland, with small, mauve flowers from July to September

Silver-studded
blue butterfly
on heather

TABLE 4.7

MEADOW GRASSES

Grass	Remarks
Annual meadow grass *Poa annua*	Greenish flowers form open, branched spires. Common on all soil types
Common bent *Agrostis tenuis*	Open, spreading flower heads, greenish or brown-purple. Widespread on acid soils
Common quaking grass *Briza media*	Handsome, flat, purple flowers drooping at the end of branches in a loose inflorescence. Often dried for decoration. Prefers dry, chalky soil
Common sedge *Carex nigra*	Male and female flowers in separate spikes on the same stem. Abundant in damp, acid soil
Crested dog's tail *Cynosurus cristatus*	Cylindrical green flower spikes with purplish anthers. Will grow in wet or dry sites
Field woodrush *Luzula campestris*	Hairy leaves and dark brown pointed flowers in clusters. Grows in dry places, with neutral to basic soil
Heath grass *Danthonia decumbens*	Tufted, with pale green flower spikes. Grows in peat heathlands or on acid sand
Meadow fescue *Festuca pratensis*	Green flower spikes in June and July. Prefers neutral clay soils
Meadow foxtail *Alopecurus pratensis*	Cylindrical flower heads with orange and purplish anthers from April to June. Common on neutral soil
Red fescue *Festuca rubra*	Green, bluish or violet-tinged flowers from May to June. Common in meadows with neutral or alkaline soil. Some forms grow on sand dunes and salt marshes
Sheep's fescue *Festuca ovina*	Densely tufted, with green, bluish or violet-tinged flower spikes in June and July. Common on dry, chalky or limy soil
Smooth meadow grass *Poa pratensis*	Loose, pyramidal flower head. Common in dry, sunny places. Prefers neutral to acid soil
Sweet vernal *Anthoxanthum odoratum*	Tufted flower heads from April to July. Gives hay its characteristic smell when cut and dried
Timothy grass *Phleum pratense*	Grey-green cylindrical inflorescences up to 20cm (8in) long. Prefers wet and heavy soil
Wall barley *Hordeum murinum*	Flowers form dense, bristly spikes, resembling those of cultivated barley in appearance
Yorkshire fog *Holcus lanatus*	Open, cream or pinkish flower heads from May to August. Very common on grassland and wasteland

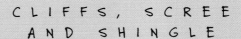

5

CLIFFS, SCREE
AND SHINGLE

Rockland habitats

Natural rockland habitats are, by their nature, less
endangered than other habitat types. Cliffs and
rocky hillsides are of little use to mankind for
building and farming, except for grazing sheep,
but that does not mean they are safe from damage.
Perhaps the greatest danger comes from the popularity
of country pursuits; walkers and rock climbers are
seriously eroding parts of beauty spots like
the Lake District. Attractive stones and rocks are
also removed from some places, legally or
illegally, for building and garden use.

ROCKLAND HISTORY

Natural rocklands are exposed and transient habitats. Coastal cliffs are battered by the sea and wind-borne sand, and in some regions are crumbling rapidly. Inland hillsides are eroded by the weather, especially from rain getting into cracks and expanding when it freezes, which causes the rock to break because of the increased pressure. Exposed to sun, constant wind and prolonged drought, it is a wonder that any life can exist there at all. Yet many plants and animals have adapted to the harsh conditions.

Close inspection of 'bare' rock reveals that it is not bare at all. All but freshly broken surfaces are covered with lichens of various types and colours. In damp and shady places, mosses and algae also grow on rocks. These primitive plants slowly cause the surface to crumble until eventually higher plants can colonize the rocks and continue this breaking-up process. The end result is soil.

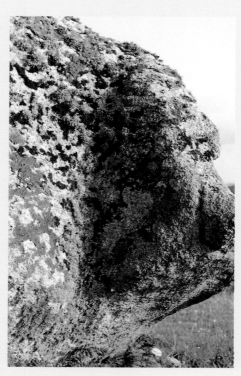

An apparently bare rock is covered with simple plants like lichens

Old stonemasonry is often colonized by mosses, lichens and algae

As rock faces begin to crumble and crack, a surprising variety of higher plants colonize soil pockets and rubble in the crevices, from small annuals to shrubs and trees. All these plants provide food and shelter for various creatures, from microbes to small mammals; these, in turn, are preyed on by carnivores.

Wall pepper flowers make bright yellow splashes on rocks and poor soil

Since mankind began making stone, brick and concrete structures, rockland life has colonized walls, roofs and roads. Lichen, mosses and algae are commonplace. Look at the roofs of urban buildings; you may see colonies of moss, lichen and maybe some higher plants growing on the tiles. Country buildings, less affected by pollution, may support rich colonies of plants. Crumbling runways of disused World War II airfields make good artificial rockland habitats; a fine example is the Norfolk Wildlife Trust's East Wretham Heath Nature Reserve, where remains of the runways and airfield buildings support large hummocks of mosses as well as various succulents and other plants of dry places.

Older walls can support more life than new ones. This is due to weathering, which produces plenty of nooks and crannies. Some old walls have a maze of tunnels inside them where small mammals live and hunt. Old neglected walls can even support trees and shrubs, and can be richer in species than are natural rocklands. This may be because there are more gaps and cracks between the bricks and stones than between natural rocks, and also that man-made features are generally more sheltered from the elements than are natural rock faces. Ruined castles, ancient stone bridges and other historic buildings are particularly valuable habitats for rockland communities.

Surveys have found that, in a typical large town, around 185 plant species grow on walls. Newer buildings, of modern materials, tend to support lichens and mosses, if anything.

GARDEN ROCKLAND HABITATS

See Table 5.1
Page 128

Most gardens already contain rockland habitats. House walls, pavements, stone ornaments, even shed and garage roofs often support a variety of lichens, mosses and other primitive plants, and even grasses, ferns and small flowering plants. Richer wildlife communities can be encouraged by specially constructed habitats.

These can take various forms. The most obvious one, perhaps, is the rockery, with large, roughly cut stones laid on the ground, often with a gravel mulch covering the bare soil between them. Most gardeners grow alpines, small conifers and trailing plants on their rockeries, but there are plenty of small native plants that are happy in these conditions.

Scree beds and seaside gardens are becoming popular, often as low-maintenance alternatives to lawns. With suitable planting, these can mimic the fallen rubble at the foot of a rock face, or a shingle beach.

Many roofs are habitats for lichens

ROCKLAND HABITAT MATERIALS

A visit to a garden centre or builders' merchant will reveal the large variety of rocks, stones and gravel available. Generally there is more choice at a garden centre, but for larger quantities a builders' merchant is cheaper. Rocks, stones and any other material, including driftwood and shells, should never be taken from the countryside or beaches: it is illegal and is threatening many wildlife sites.

For rockeries and walls, two main types of material are widely available: sandstone and limestone. Sandstone comes in shades of brown, red, orange, yellow, grey and white. Its soft, rough surface is quickly colonized by mosses and lichens. The stone absorbs moisture and may flake in frosty weather.

Limestone varies in colour and texture depending on where it was quarried. Types include Cotswold, Derbyshire and Westmoreland and the colour may be white, cream, grey, brown or nearly black. Harder than sandstone, it weathers well. Limestone walls and rockeries limit the choice of plants to those which like well-drained, limy soil. It is attacked by airborne acids, and this may be a problem in areas of high atmospheric pollution, though this is much less likely today than it used to be, due to restrictions on domestic coal fires and industrial processes which pollute the air with acidic substances.

For scree and shingle beds there is a variety of materials, shapes, sizes and colours available. Cobbles – stones and pebbles that have been worn into smooth round shapes by the action of water – come in sizes ranging from large boulders to small pea gravel; these are particularly good for seaside gardens, as they resemble a pebble beach.

Flint is a hard and brittle rock and has a dark, shiny surface when broken. It occurs naturally in regions with chalk bedrock. Flint fragments make attractive walls, rockeries and scree beds.

There are various sizes and colours of gravel, including pink, white, green, fawn, brown and mixed. The more exotic colours are expensive but make an attractive small scree bed. Broken slates, which come in grey, green or blue, also make decorative scree beds.

If you are planning to build a wall in or around your garden, you might consider dry stone walling. This can be long-lasting and substantial – farmers have been building them in the countryside for centuries – and the gaps between the stones can support a wealth of plants and small creatures. Even 'normal' brick walls and pavements can play a part in

Garden ornaments soon become covered with almost invisible
lichens, algae and mosses

supporting rockland wildlife. Paths and drives, for instance, whether gravel or paved, can be planted with low-growing species which do not mind being walked on or even driven on occasionally; this is a useful way of including a habitat in a small garden where space is at a premium.

WALLS

Walls are long-term features of a garden, whether they mark a boundary or separate garden rooms, screen ugly sights, or retain a tier or raised bed. Walls used for any of these functions can be constructed in such a way that they also act as wildlife habitats. Usually the positions and types of walls are considered at the planning stage of a garden. Walls can easily be introduced into an established garden, however, and they do not have to be very big; my own dry stone wall is about 30cm (12in) high, and edges a small, raised woodland area.

A dry stone wall is the most useful type for sheltering wildlife. Flattish stones of various sizes are required; these must be easy to lay on top of one another, and stay in place without mortar. The best way to build a wall for wildlife is to stack the stones randomly, leaving lots of gaps where plants can grow and animals can shelter.

Another attractive wall style consists of flint pieces stuck into cement. Buildings and walls in many seaside areas are built in this way. We have such a wall, which my husband built only a few years ago, in a corner of our own garden. This is already half covered with ivy, algae and spiders' webs, and visitors tell us how lucky we are to have part of an ancient ruin in our garden!

A good way to make a flint wall is to build a sub-structure of breeze blocks or cheap bricks for strength, then coat this with cement and insert the stones before the cement dries. An existing wall can also be coated with flints in this way.

BUILDING A DRY STONE WALL

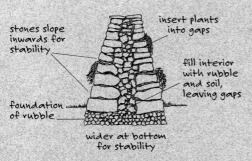

stones slope inwards for stability

insert plants into gaps

fill interior with rubble and soil, leaving gaps

foundation of rubble

wider at bottom for stability

A free-standing dry stone wall should be wider at the bottom, with lots of crevices

Dry stone walls can be either free-standing or retaining, but in either case should be laid on a foundation of sand, hard core or concrete, depending on the height and position of the wall.

A free-standing wall should taper from bottom to top, with the width at the base equal to about half the height. Place any larger stones towards the bottom and build it up in layers. The stones should lean slightly downwards towards the centre for stability. Fill in the centre with rubble, stones and some earth, making sure there are plenty of gaps for plants and small creatures to colonize.

A retaining wall, used to support a raised border or terrace, should be built leaning backwards towards the retained ground, with the stones jammed into the soil behind. If the ground behind the wall is wet, drainage will be needed to prevent frost damage. Narrow clay or plastic pipes, set at intervals near the bottom of the wall and extending about 30cm (12in) into the soil, will solve this problem. If there are plenty of gaps between the stones and the soil is free-draining, extra drainage should not be necessary.

Both free-standing and retaining walls can be interplanted while they are being built. For this, pack soil between the stones like mortar and place small, container-grown plants into it, on their sides.

Primitive plants, such as lichens, mosses, algae and liverworts, will soon appear on a new wall, turning the surface into a mosaic of colours and textures. Such colonization can be speeded up by painting the stones' exposed surfaces with a thin paste of flour and milk, with a little liquid manure added. Within a few months the wall will be flourishing with multicoloured species.

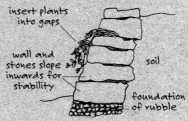

insert plants into gaps

wall and stones slope inwards for stability

soil

foundation of rubble

A dry stone wall can be used to edge a tier or raised flowerbed

Even a more formal wall can provide a valuable habitat, supporting animals and plants on its surface and in gaps between the stones or bricks. Old, weathered bricks are colonized more quickly by mosses and lichens than new ones, so get hold of these if you can. Homes for spiders and other small creatures can be made by drilling small holes in the brickwork with a masonry drill; these will soon be occupied. You may like to leave a few gaps between the bricks to fill with soil and plant with ferns or trailing plants.

Flint walls have lots of crannies for spiders, snails and other small animals to shelter in

Many types of small plants can be planted into a wall. The most spectacular varieties are those which trail and spread, partly covering the stones and providing extra shelter for small creatures. Ivy can be allowed to scramble up a wall, providing shelter for larger creatures like butterflies and birds.

ROCKERIES

It is generally recommended that a rock garden should be in a sunny spot away from overhanging trees. That is because the alpines and other small plants normally grown on rockeries prefer these conditions. A rockland habitat, on the other hand, need not keep to these constraints; after all, cliffs and hillsides can have any aspect, and be in the open or sheltered by trees. Obviously, different conditions attract different wildlife.

A rockery should be on a slope. If you have a natural slope in your garden, this is the best place, but if not, a free-standing mound can be constructed. Rock gardens are often built by ponds and streams, or to edge tiers or raised beds.

A rockery should mimic a natural outcrop. Before starting one, inspect natural hillsides, if possible. Often the rocks are in layers, following the contours of the hillside. A natural-looking rock garden should be built similarly, rather than placing stones at random.

MAKING A ROCKERY

gritty soil

rocks slope
into the soil
for stability

foundation of rubble
for good drainage

This section of a free-standing rockery shows how rocks
should slope inwards so that rain flows into the soil

Rockeries need very good drainage: many rockland plants tend to rot at soil level if they are wet for any length of time. If your soil is heavy, break it up and add plenty of grit or rubble. A free-standing rockery can be built on a pile of rubble, for added bulk, covered with soil.

Use stones in proportion to your site. For a rock feature, a few larger stones look more effective than many smaller ones. Keep the design simple or the rockery will look fussy and overcrowded.

Plants can be introduced as soon as the rockery is ready. When they are in place, mulch the soil with a good layer of chippings or gravel of the same material as the rocks; this suppresses weeds, reduces the risk of stem rot in delicate species, and looks more natural than bare earth.

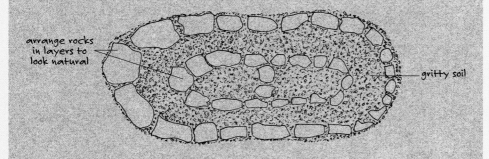

arrange rocks
in layers to
look natural

gritty soil

A rockery looks more natural when the rocks are placed
in layers, following the contours of each stone

Natural rocks form in layers

Garden rockeries should be built in layers to look natural

Local stone is best. As well as being cheaper, because of low transport costs, and more readily available, it will suit the local wildlife better. This is because rocks are not inert, but affect what grows near them. Limestone, for example, makes the surrounding soil alkaline, which favours some plants but prevents others from growing well, if at all.

Rockery plants should be in scale, and mostly ground-hugging and tussock-forming types; remember that in the wild, these plants would be exposed to the elements and stunted in their growth. As a number of rock plants tend to rot at the base of the stem, the soil should be very well drained.

SCREE AND SHINGLE BEDS

Scree and shingle beds are flatter versions of rockeries; they can be on a gentle slope, but not too steep or the gravel will roll off them. They mimic the broken stones (scree) that lie at the foot of rocky cliffs, gravel beds deposited by streams, and shingle beaches.

Natural scree beds are usually in the open, but they can have any aspect. This means that a scree habitat can be in sun or partial shade. It is best to avoid overhanging trees, mainly because it is awkward to rake fallen leaves off gravel.

Like rockeries, scree beds need very well-drained soil, so dig in plenty of grit if your ground is not naturally free draining. A thick layer of gravel – at least 8cm (3in) – is needed to suppress weeds and reduce the risk of stem rot in your rock plants: gravel around the stems drains quickly, so helps to keep them dry. You could lay a porous plastic membrane before placing the gravel; this would keep weeds down but, adversely, would prevent your chosen plants from self-seeding and spreading.

Many types, colours and sizes of gravel are available; as for rockeries, it is best to buy local material, although some interesting and ornamental effects can be produced using unusually coloured gravel on a small scale.

Of course, a scree bed can be made next to a rockery for a natural look. A stand-alone scree bed is obviously not natural, and can be formal or informal in shape: the wildlife will not know the difference. You could place a few larger pebbles, rocks or stepping stones to decorate the bed.

Tussock-forming plants and small shrubs mixed with self-seeding annuals look good in a scree bed. Vigorous, spreading plants are best avoided or they will soon cover the entire area.

Seaside shingle gardens are similar to scree beds. Use rounded gravel and stones of various sizes and colours for a natural effect, perhaps with some pieces of driftwood and sea shells scattered around. Grow predominantly coastal wildflowers in this type of habitat.

PAVEMENTS

Gardeners are often annoyed by weeds growing in the gaps between paving stones, but this can be put to advantage by converting part of your paving into a rockland habitat. If never or seldom walked on, paving becomes coated with mosses and lichens (take care: mossy paving is slippery when wet). My next-door neighbour's back yard, untended for several years, has a thick patch of moss growing on the concrete path in one shady corner, and both wild and garden plants growing in the cracks, including grass, plantain, dandelion, hoary mullein, eryngium (related to sea holly), violet, sun spurge and scarlet pimpernel.

You could remove paving slabs at random and plant low-growing varieties, like thyme or thrift, which don't mind being trodden on occasionally; fill the planting hole with gritty soil or compost and put a layer of gravel on top.

ROCKLAND PLANTS

See Table 5.2
Page 129

Table 5.2 suggests small native or naturalized plants that like rockland conditions, but you could try anything which likes free-draining soil. For a coastal shingle habitat, many of the plants of sand dunes (see Table 4.5, page 109) are suitable.

Many successful rockland plants are annuals which grow rapidly and seed themselves in a season. Others are biennials and perennials with long, narrow roots which spread wide and deep in search of water. Some have small, narrow or hairy leaves to reduce water loss, while others are succulent, storing water in their leaves.

Some annuals which may naturally colonize your rockland include shepherd's purse, groundsel, mouse-eared chickweed and rue-leaved saxifrage. Their seeds are light and are carried by wind; if they are deposited in crevices they can lodge and germinate. Succulent colonizers include stonecrop varieties and navelwort.

PLANTING A ROCKLAND HABITAT

Plants are best introduced as container-grown specimens. Annuals can be bought or grown from seed in small pots. Water the plants well in their pots before planting. To plant in a rockery or scree bed, move aside the gravel, remove some soil and place the root ball in the hole. Water the plant and replace the gravel mulch. The plant should quickly become established and need little further attention.

pot-grown plants can be inserted sideways between stones, then packed in with soil or compost

Saxifrages and some other rock plants rot if rainwater is trapped in their rosettes, so these are happier if planted sideways in rock clefts or dry stone walls. To do this, stuff the root ball into place, packing extra soil around it. This is easier said than done and can be messy, frustrating and rather fun; wet the soil first to make it sticky so that it stays in place. Once established, annuals, biennials and some perennials seed themselves readily.

MAINTENANCE OF ROCKLAND HABITATS

Rockland habitats need very little maintenance. The wildflowers can be allowed to seed themselves and spread, and it is easy to pull up excess seedlings and cut back perennials if they spread too much. Occasional weeds will need removing. Rock plants develop very long roots which go deep in search of water and nutrients. It is not necessary ever to feed or water rock plants once they are established; in fact, they grow much better if left to their own devices.

Ivy-leaved toadflax has an unusual adaptation. When pollinated, its flowers develop an aversion to light. Their stalks lengthen, carrying the ripening seed capsules to the darkest places they can reach and depositing them in crevices, the most suitable places for them to germinate. Several fern varieties, including Hart's-tongue and rusty-back, colonize walls.

ROCKLAND WILDLIFE

As the plants become established, animals move in. Hunting spiders, woodlice, ants, beetles, slugs and snails lurk in the stones of a rockery or dry stone wall, attracting predatory birds. Broken snail shells provide evidence of thrushes at work; they crack the shells on the stones to expose the snails' soft bodies.

Rocks, bricks, stone and concrete all absorb heat more efficiently than does soil, and radiate it through the night like a storage heater. This microclimate attracts butterflies and moths which enjoy the warmth from the stones, even when the weather is cool.

Solitary bumblebees and other insects make nests in narrow gaps between stones, laying their eggs out of harm's way. You can encourage these creatures by inserting bundles of hollow stems or drinking straws among the stones, giving them shelter and a place to hide. Stems and straws may also attract groups of hibernating ladybirds: they hide inside the hollow stems of herbacious perennials and use straws in the same way. Reptiles such as slow worms and common lizards may take up residence, basking on the warm rocks on a sunny day.

The gaps and tunnels inside a dry stone wall are a maze where voles, mice and shrews hunt invertebrates. These may themselves be preyed on by weasels, whose slender bodies can squeeze through small spaces. Many small birds, including house sparrows, tits and flycatchers, nest or roost in walls. Wrens and dunnocks are small enough to hunt insects in the cavities.

As the plants spread, they provide further havens for invertebrates, behind and underneath them; ivy growing on a wall, for instance, can shelter small birds, butterflies and spiders.

The plants themselves support dependent creatures. Many wall plants flower in late spring and, as well as producing a colourful display, provide valuable early nectar and pollen for bees, butterflies and moths.

Even the primitive rockland plants belong to food chains; woodlice, millipedes and some types of molluscs and caterpillars graze on the algae growing on damp walls.

Some rockland inhabitants are microscopic: springtails, nematodes and rotifers feed on lichens, mosses and detritus. Like their food plants, these creatures can shrivel up in dry conditions and revive when it rains again.

Small creatures, like these banded snails, hide in gaps between stones and rocks

TABLE 5.1

ROCKS, STONES AND GRAVEL

Material	Uses	Advantages	Disadvantages
Sandstone	Walls, rockeries	Attractive colour and texture	Soft, can be affected by frost
Limestone	Walls, rockeries	Good colour, weathers well	Limited to lime-loving plants. May be corroded by air pollution
Flint	Walls, rockeries, scree and shingle beds	Attractive colour and texture, weathers well	
Bricks	Walls	Sturdy and versatile; old, recycled bricks quite cheap	Bricks with smooth surfaces very slow to acquire mosses and lichens. Some bricks are not frost-hardy
Cobbles (rounded stones)	Rockeries, shingle beds	Variety of colours, textures and sizes	
Pea gravel (rounded gravel)	Scree and shingle beds, drives and paths	Variety of colours and sizes	Needs confining to bed or path by edging
Gravel	Scree beds, drives and paths, mulching rockeries	Variety of colours and sizes; suppresses weeds	Needs confining to bed or path by edging. Some colours are expensive
Slate fragments	Scree beds, mulching rockeries	Variety of colours	Expensive

TABLE 5.2

ROCKLAND PLANTS

Plant	Remarks
Herb robert *Geranium robertianum*	Small annual. Hairy red stems and dissected leaves. Small pink flowers all summer. Popular with bees. Common in woodland clearings, hedge bottoms, dry stone walls and coastal shingle
Ivy-leaved toadflax *Cymbalaria muralis*	Trailing plant. Mauve, yellow and pink flower spikes, like small antirrhinums, May to September. Compact varieties 'Globosa' and 'Globosa rosea' make neat tufts 15–19cm (6–8in) across
Pink *Dianthus* varieties	Dwarf varieties include the rare Cheddar pink (*D. gratianopolitanus*), common pink (*D. plumarius*), and maiden pink (*D. deltoides*). Pinks need neutral or limy soil. They attract bees, butterflies and moths
Purple mountain saxifrage *Saxifraga oppositifolia*	Cushions of tiny leaves. Produces masses of purple flowers in early spring, attracting bees and butterflies
Rock rose *Helianthemum nummularium*	Small shrub with pale yellow flowers from June to September. Attractive to bees and other insects. Found on chalk downs and shingle banks
Spring gentian *Gentiana verna*	Rare annual, with blue spring flowers. Attractive to butterflies and bees
Stonecrop *Sedum album*	Prostrate succulent, with erect white flower heads in July
Thrift *Armeria maritima*	Evergreen perennial, common on sandy cliffs. Resembles tiny pinks, with pink or white flowers in summer
Wall pennywort *Cotyledon umbilicus-veneris*	Perennial with succulent circular leaves. Flowering stems in summer produce green-white, drooping flowers. Common in rock crevices and walls in mild, damp regions
Wall pepper *Sedum acre*	Mat of creeping stems and flat heads of bright yellow, starry flowers in June and July
Wallflower *Cheiranthus cheiri*	Biennial or short-lived perennial. Freely produced, fragrant, red, orange or yellow flowers in late spring, visited by bees. Dwarf varieties are available. Established on old walls in places

Herb robert

Thrift

6

P O T T E D   H O M E S

Container habitats

It is possible to create all habitat types in containers. This means that people with paved back yards, even balconies and roof gardens, can participate in wildlife gardening. Containers are also easier for those who find it difficult or impossible to bend down. Container habitats are not just for the gardenless and disabled, however. (See Advantages of container habitats, page 132.)

ADVANTAGES OF CONTAINER HABITATS

- They are ideal for sites without soil such as paved yards, balconies, roof gardens and window ledges.

- They can be very small, and hence fit into small spaces.

- They are easier for disabled and elderly gardeners to maintain as they are generally set higher than ground level, and hence require less bending and stooping.

- Small plants are easier to see in containers than when planted in the ground.

- Containers confine vigorously spreading plants, which is particularly important for marsh habitats, where plants can spread rapidly.

- They allow a greater variety of habitats; you are not constrained by your garden's soil type and other local conditions.

- You can fit more habitat types into a given space.

- They make very attractive features.

See Table 6.1
Page 145

Pink campions and white daisies make a pretty display which would be perfect for an ornamental container

ORNAMENTAL WILDFLOWERS

Many wildflowers are attractive enough to be grown in containers simply for their ornamental value, and are also important bee and butterfly plants. I often make colourful summer displays in large plastic containers, simply by sowing a mixture of annual wildflower seeds.

Unwin's mixed flowers for butterflies is a good selection; it includes a variety of wildflowers like cornflower and poppy, with small garden annuals like candytuft. Many of the varieties listed in the tables in

Containers of ornamental flowers provide nectar for insects

Chapters 2–5 can be used, but Table 6.1 brings together a selection of decorative wildflowers which can be grown in ornamental containers, either with other wildflowers or mixed with garden varieties like tagetes and petunias.

MINIATURE HABITATS

More interesting and valuable, and just as attractive in their own way, are wildlife habitats in miniature, as they re-create, as far as possible, the conditions found in nature, perhaps introducing some less flamboyant plants. We shall now look at different ways of creating various habitat types in containers.

WOODLANDS

A woodland in a pot sounds even more incredible than a small woodland habitat in a garden. There is great scope in planting up a woodland container, however. A tub can be used for a forest tree, for example. This may seem strange, but the Japanese have been doing it for centuries on an even smaller scale. Bonsai, growing miniature trees in

See Table 6.2 Page 146

containers, involves keeping the plants small by judicious pruning and training. The trees used are normal varieties, not special dwarf types.

A normally large tree, such as an oak, ash, beech or hornbeam, can easily be grown in a container. Because trees use a lot of water, small containers may need watering several times daily in hot weather. To cut down on the need to water, use as large a tub as possible and mix water-retaining granules with the compost. Use good soil or a soil-based compost, and feed the tree weekly during the growing season. Cover the surface with leaf mould or bark chippings to suppress weeds.

TYPES OF CONTAINERS

There is a tremendous variety of containers available from garden centres and shops, in different materials, sizes, shapes, colours and prices. Which ones are suitable for container wildlife habitats? All of them! As with any container display, it depends on your personal taste. Ornate ceramic pots, for instance, can be planted with colour co-ordinated, decorative wildflowers to rival any bedding display. If you prefer your habitats to look more natural, go for plain wood, stone, concrete or terracotta.

Plastic containers have much improved over the years; it is now difficult to distinguish good plastic imitations from real terracotta, stone or other materials. Plastic is relatively cheap and lightweight, and is good for most habitat types except, perhaps, those which need very good drainage, like rockland and seaside habitats.

Wood is another versatile material. Wooden containers range from large – and expensive – half barrels, to small, light, and cheap tubs, hanging baskets and window boxes. Some are sold in pieces to be self-assembled. If you enjoy woodwork, you can easily make your own wooden containers, limited only by your ability and imagination!

Recently, metal containers have become popular. These look great, but heat up and cool down very quickly, and so are limited in what they can grow. They are best suited to wetland habitats – ponds and bogs – as water is slow to warm and cool, and acts as a heat reservoir.

Containers do not have to be large to hold a habitat. A single plant in an attractive pot will still attract its dependent insects and play a role in the conservation of the local ecology.

To keep the tree small, prune it regularly. Remove a third of the older branches every year in late winter, and your tree should last many years.

Many native shrubs and small trees can be grown in tubs. Hawthorn, blackthorn, elder and the evergreen native privet all have cream flowers in spring or early summer, which attract butterflies, moths and bees, followed by colourful, juicy berries which feed blackbirds and thrushes in autumn. Hazel has yellow catkins early in the year and edible nuts in autumn. Holly is evergreen; there are many variegated forms, and female varieties produce red, orange or yellow berries if there is a nearby male to pollinate the flowers.

Small trees and shrubs generally need less pruning than potentially large ones. Hazel and elder can be coppiced, and the others can be clipped with shears to keep them from outgrowing their space. Topiary can even be practised on holly and privet. Over-cutting any of these varieties, however, tends to reduce the amount of flowers and fruits they produce.

Containers made of wood, either natural or stained brown, look great for woodland habitats. Half barrels are excellent. There is a good variety of smaller wooden containers available, including hollowed-out logs which are ideal for small spaces. Treat wooden containers with a plant-friendly preservative if you want them to last.

Woodland wildflowers

Small containers, including window boxes and hanging baskets, can be planted with a variety of small woodland wildflowers; any of those featured in Table 2.4 (see page 55) are worth trying. Many ferns will grow in woodland containers, their lacy foliage making an attractive display. Evergreen trailers like ivy and periwinkle are good for hanging baskets and window boxes; there are variegated versions for year-round interest.

See Table 2.4
Page 55

Most woodland floor plants flower in spring, before deciduous trees come into leaf and block the sunlight, so your container will do best in a semi-shaded position. Use a humus-rich compost, such as one made from coir or bark chippings, add water-retaining granules, and keep well watered.

See Table 6.3
Page 147

Woodland flowers are important nectar and pollen providers for early bees and butterflies, and provide colourful and unusual displays before the summer bedding blooms.

PONDS

Any waterproof container can easily be used to make a small pond, either free-standing or submerged. For submerged pools the container is buried in the ground and hence is barely visible, so plastic buckets and bowls can be used. For a free-standing pond, use an attractive container made of glazed ceramic, plastic or metal. A wooden half-barrel makes an interesting water feature; when wet the wood swells and makes the barrel waterproof – after all, it was originally designed to hold ale. I once used an old enamel sink, which looked okay once algae and lichens started to grow on the outside.

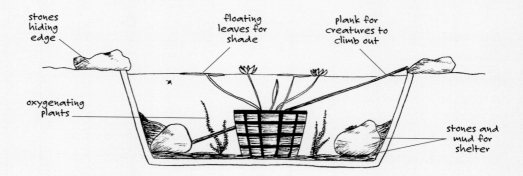

stones hiding edge

floating leaves for shade

plank for creatures to climb out

oxygenating plants

stones and mud for shelter

A ground-level wildlife pond in a plastic bowl

Containers that are not waterproof, including those made of clay (unless glazed), stone or concrete, most wooden ones and, of course, anything with drainage holes, can be lined with a small piece of plastic pond liner, although this can be a fiddly job if the container is small or strangely shaped.

Wetland containers, except very small ones, are heavy and difficult to move, so make sure yours is in the right spot before filling it. Put a small quantity of soil in the bottom, add some shingle and a few pebbles, and fill with water.

See Tables 3.2–3.4
Pages 80–2

A larger container can be planted with a variety of aquatics, including submerged oxygenators, floating-leaved plants, and marginals. Many of the plants included in Tables 3.2, 3.3 and 3.4 (see pages 80, 81 and 82) are suitable, depending on the size of your container. To keep the water fresh and aerated, plant a slow-growing oxygenator like water milfoil (myriophyllum) or water starwort (callitriche). Dwarf water lilies (*Nymphaea pygmaea* vars.) will not grow too vigorously. Place pots of small marginals around the edge, standing them on bricks, if necessary, to bring them up to the correct height.

Your container pond will soon attract diving beetles, water spiders, pond skaters and other invertebrates. You may find that interesting creatures, such as water fleas, water shrimps, flatworms, leeches and aquatic insect larvae, have been introduced on the water plants.

It is unlikely that animals will fall into a free-standing pond, but if you have a steep-sided, buried pond, it is important to put a sloping plank of wood or pile of pebbles against the side, so that any creature that falls in can climb out again. Frogs and newts may visit and even spawn in such a pond. Birds will drink and bathe in shallow container ponds, whether at ground level or raised.

See Table 3.4 Page 82

An alternative way to grow decorative marginal plants is to have a single specimen in a small ceramic or plastic container. Place the plant, in its pot, in the container, on a brick if necessary, then fill the container to the brim with water. Add a piece of charcoal to keep the water fresh in the absence of oxygenators; it will absorb impurities. As well as the varieties given in Table 3.4 (see page 82), you can grow some of the more vigorous marginals in this way; yellow flag iris (*Iris pseudacorus*), bog rush (*Juncus glaucus*) and arrowhead (*Sagittaria sagittifolia*), for example, would soon take over a small pond but can easily be grown in a container. I have used a group of three ceramic pots, each with a different water plant, to good effect.

One major problem with water in a ceramic container is that it may freeze and break the pot in winter. Unless you live in a mild, sheltered area, the water should be emptied out when sub-zero temperatures are forecast; the plants, whose top-growth will have died back, can be over-wintered in a shed or cold greenhouse.

MARSHLANDS

Many beautiful, and in some cases endangered, marshland wildflowers can be grown in containers that have few or no drainage holes. These containers look more natural with a mixture of species grown together. For example, ragged robin (*Lychnis flos-cuculi*), lady's smock (*Cardamine pratensis*), water forget-me-not (*Myosotis scorpioides*) water mint (*Mentha aquatica*) and bugle (*Ajuga reptans*) would make an unusual and pleasing display.

Marshland flowers, like this forget-me-not, are just as good at attracting insects whether grown in containers or in the wild

The soil or compost should be kept moist but not water-logged; add water-retaining granules before planting up.

MEADOWS

For a colourful temporary display, grow a mixture of cornfield annuals (poppy, cornflower, corncockle and corn marigold) from seed.

More permanent meadows can be sown from seed mixtures, or individual plants can be inserted. A mixture of flowers looks best. For a spring meadow container, try cowslip (*Primula veris*), snake's-head fritillary (*Fritillaria meleagris*), lady's smock (*Cardamine pratensis*), and self-heal (*Prunella vulgaris*). Any of the spring bulbs in Table 4.2 (see page 106) can be grown in containers.

See Table 4.2
Page 106

A summer grassland container might include varieties such as field scabious (*Knautia arvensis*), knapweed (*Centaurea scabiosa*), meadow buttercup (*Ranunculus acris*), harebell (*Campanula rotundifolia*) and oxeye daisy (*Leucanthemum vulgare*). Include some non-vigorous grasses and allow them to flower.

Practically any container can be used to create a meadow. Use poor soil or a soil-based compost such as John Innes No. 1. Add water-retaining granules to reduce the need for watering, especially in small containers. Drainage should be good, so ensure there are sufficient drainage holes.

A perennial container meadow needs to be harvested annually. Trim a spring meadow in July, and a summer meadow in September, using shears for both.

A beautiful swallowtail butterfly sipping nectar from a speedwell

Grass flowers are attractive enough for container meadows

'JUNK' CONTAINERS

If you can spare some time going round car-boot sales, second-hand shops, market stalls and scrap yards, you will come across a variety of discarded items which can be bought cheaply and used as unusual containers. These may include old sinks, baths, buckets, toilets, chimney pots, kitchen appliances, wellington boots and many other things. You may even have such things already, in the attic or garden shed, or left behind by builders.

With some imagination, unusual and attractive displays can be made by planting up these containers with native and naturalized plants.

To give you an idea, I have in my own garden, amongst other items, a zinc bath salvaged from a neighbour's garden, a metal bucket from a car-boot sale, a chimneypot from the house roof, and a clay drain junction which I found behind the garage. The chimneypot now contains a woodland habitat, namely a variegated periwinkle (*Vinca minor*). Because my soil is alkaline sand, and hence, if I want a heathland habitat I can only grow it in a container, I have filled the drainage junction with ericaceous compost and planted it with heathers.

Recently I spotted an innovative container in a small front garden. A shallow trough had been placed on an old sowing machine treadle table and filled with water and a few aquatic plants; very unusual.

HEATHLANDS

Acid heath plants, most of which are small shrubs, will grow happily in containers in the right conditions. Use an ericaceous (acid) compost with water-retaining granules. Water only with rainwater – tap water contains lime, which is alkaline, while rainwater is slightly acid, which suits acid heath plants – and never let the compost dry out because it is difficult to re-wet. Any container is suitable, as long as it has good drainage and does not become waterlogged. Place it in an open position in full sun if possible.

Any of the small heathland plants included in Table 4.6 (see page 110) can be used. They should be clipped lightly after flowering to prevent them from getting woody and straggly.

See Table 4.6
Page 110

ROCKLANDS

Alpine troughs are popular garden features. Rocky hillsides and scree beds can be mimicked by similarly growing rock plants in stone or concrete troughs. An alternative container is an old enamel sink coated with rough concrete; this looks like stone when it sets, especially when it has acquired some lichens on its surface. Terracotta pots also make good containers for smaller rocklands.

TUFA

Although not strictly a container, because the plants are outside it rather than inside, a piece of tufa rock can provide the foundation of an unusual, small rockland habitat.

Tufa is a limestone-based rock that is very light, soft and porous. There are a few small rock plants which enjoy dry conditions that can grow in the cavities in tufa. Simply push a little gritty compost into the cavities and insert the plants. If you need more or bigger cavities, use a masonry drill to make them.

Plants to try include herb robert (*Geranium robertianum*), stonecrop (*Sedum* spp.), pink varieties (*Dianthus* spp.) and saxifrages (*Saxifraga* spp.). Mosses and lichens also grow well on tufa. Avoid acid lovers.

Once the plants are established they should need little tending. If they flag in dry weather, dowse the rock with rainwater from a watering can. This will produce a fine spray which is less likely to disturb the precariously held plants than water from a hose or poured from a jug, though a jug could be used with care.

MAKING AN IMITATION STONE TROUGH

It is easy to make an authentic-looking stone container – and for much less cost than buying one – by coating something with concrete. Suitable items include polystyrene boxes, plastic bowls and buckets, old sinks and cheap plastic tubs, to name just a few.

Using two cardboard boxes as a mould, it is easy to make an imitation 'stone' trough from concrete

The surface to be coated should be clean and rough to improve the adhesion of the concrete, so rub any smooth surfaces with sandpaper or steel wool. Mix three parts coarse sand with one part cement (add a little fine gravel to make a rougher surface if required), then add a little water and slap the stiff mixture onto the surface. Don't worry too much about smoothing the concrete surface: it looks more natural when left rough. When it has dried it will be difficult to tell it from the real thing.

Another way to make a 'stone' trough from concrete is to use two sturdy cardboard boxes, one slightly smaller than the other. Pour a thick concrete mix into the bottom of the larger box to make a layer a few centimetres deep, and insert a piece of chicken wire or nylon netting into it for reinforcement. Next, place the smaller box inside the larger and pour concrete into the gap between the two, again adding reinforcing mesh. This is a fiddly job. Place the mesh in the gap between the boxes, then start pouring in the concrete. The trick is to keep the wire in the middle of the cavity, so you may need to hold and adjust it until the gap is almost full. Leave to set, then remove the boxes; the cardboard should pull off quite easily once the concrete is dry. Drainage holes, if required, can be drilled with a masonry drill when the concrete has set.

Container rocklands can be placed in full sun or partial shade, as required by the plant varieties growing in them.

Good drainage is vital for container rocklands – drill extra drainage holes if there are not enough. Place a good layer of bulky material, such as coarse stones or rubble, on the bottom of the container; the polystyrene used for packing, and vermiculite, perlite or perlag (natural minerals heat-treated to give them a honeycomb-like structure) are lightweight alternatives. Top this with a mixture of equal parts loam or soil-based compost, leaf mould and horticultural grit, leaving a gap of about 3cm (1¼in) between it and the container top. Place rocks and large pebbles on the surface, insert the plants, then cover the surface with a layer of gravel, preferably the same colour as the stones.

A suitable mixture of plants for a container rockery might include herb robert (*Geranium robertianum*), stonecrop (*Sedum album*), harebell (*Campanula rotundifolia*), and ivy-leaved toadflax (*Cymbalaria muralis*) with a small-leaved ivy (*Hedera helix*) trailing over the edge. Table 5.2 (see page 129) lists other suitable plants.

See Table 5.2
Page 129

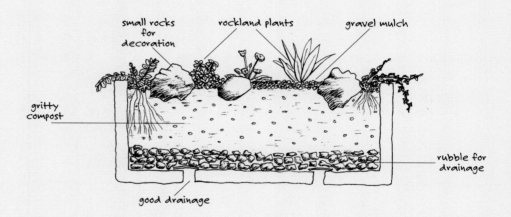

A rockland habitat in a stone trough or old sink

SEASIDE HABITATS

Plants of sand dunes and shingle beaches can be grown in containers in a similar way to plants of rocky hillsides. Stone, concrete, terracotta or plain wood containers are suitable, and should be sited in full sun if possible. As for container rocklands, place a layer of coarse material on the bottom to improve drainage. Use a sandy soil or compost and top with a layer of small pea shingle mixed with a few larger pebbles. An interesting piece of driftwood or some shells add a nice finishing touch. Plant with small coastal varieties like thrift (*Armeria maritima*), dog violet (*Viola canina*), wall pepper (*Sedum acre*) and Hottentot fig (*Carpobrotus edulis*), or any of the varieties listed in Table 4.5 (see page 109).

See Table 4.5
Page 109

HANGING BASKETS AND WINDOW BOXES

liner

trailing plant
to hide
basket edges

plants can
be planted
through holes
in the liner

open mesh
basket

Small wildflowers can be grown in a hanging basket

Containers that are raised off the ground are only seen from underneath. These include hanging baskets, wall-mounted pots and pouches, and window boxes on upstairs ledges. Trailing plants are important in these. The most obvious habitat is woodland, in which climbers like ivy and periwinkle are allowed to hang down.

Open-mesh wire or plastic hanging baskets can be planted through the sides and the top, extending the range of plants that can be used. These baskets need a liner: moss (bought or from your lawn, not gathered from the countryside), black polythene, coir matting, even an old jumper or T-shirt, can be used – the plants will soon cover it up. Ornamental woodland and meadow wildflowers can then be planted. Use a soil-less compost for its light weight, water the plants regularly and never let the compost dry out. You could also try rockland plants like thrift (*Armeria maritima*), which grows on sandy cliffs, stonecrops (*Sedum* spp.), small pinks (*Dianthus* spp.) and other small wildflowers of cliffs and walls. These prefer well-drained soil, so add light-weight perlite or vermiculite to the compost. There is no reason why plants from any habitat, except wetland, because of the weight, cannot be grown in hanging baskets.

Window boxes on ledges are supported underneath so can hold more weight. You could grow marshland plants in a plastic trough with no holes, keeping them well watered. Even a window-ledge mini-pond is possible. Use pot-grown marginals and fill the trough with water. As water is very heavy, please ensure your window wetland is well secured and can take the weight, or those underneath may get a surprise!

MAINTENANCE OF CONTAINER HABITATS

Different container habitats need different maintenance regimes, depending mainly on the plants grown in them. Shrubs and small trees make long-term displays, lasting years or even decades. These need watering daily during the growing season, and more in hot, dry weather; never let them dry out. They also need feeding with a soluble organic fertilizer such as liquid manure or seaweed extract. Every spring, remove the top few inches of compost and replace with fresh, adding water-retaining granules and a sprinkling of solid fertilizer such as blood, fish and bone. Prune the plants to keep them a reasonable size and shape; remove any dead and diseased wood first, then about one-third of the older growth. Deciduous shrubs and trees are dormant in winter, but evergreens are at risk of freezing during cold spells and drying out in strong winds. Keep them in a sheltered place, and in cold weather, wrap their pots in hessian, bubble-polythene or some other insulating material to prevent their roots from freezing – this could kill the plant.

Most other container habitats are relatively short-term and need renewing regularly to keep them looking their best. With careful tending, you might keep a meadow for several years, harvesting it annually to favour the flowers over the grasses. Eventually one or more of the plants will begin to dominate the others. When this happens, lift these plants, split them and replant a few of the outer portions to replace the old plants. Some potted habitats, such as cornfields, are intended to last only one growing season.

Marshland plants are often vigorous and may need dividing and replanting every year or two. Container ponds, on the other hand, often need little maintenance. Plants may outgrow their space and need thinning and dividing every few years. It all depends on the varieties you grow. Wetlands in clay or ceramic containers must be prevented from freezing in winter or the pressure from the ice will crack the pots.

Apart from shrubs and trees, container habitats do not need feeding, particularly if the wildflowers are to grow well: feeding encourages foliage to grow strongly at the expense of flowers, and may lead to pest and disease problems.

Container meadows, heaths, bogs and ponds must never dry out; water them regularly during summer and any dry spell. Tap water is fine for meadows and woodlands, but use rainwater for heathland habitats as tap water contains dissolved alkaline salts, and heathland requires acid conditions. Rainwater is also best for wetland habitats as it contains none of the nitrates and other fertilizers which result in green algal growth.

TABLE 6.1

ORNAMENTAL WILDFLOWERS SUITABLE FOR CONTAINERS

Plant	Habitat type	Remarks
Bluebell *Hyacinthoides non-scripta**	Woodland	Spring bulb. Scented blue, pink or white flowers. Damp soil in dappled shade
Corn marigold *Chrysanthemum segetum*	Cornfield	Annual. Orange-yellow daisy-like flowers. Full sun
Corncockle *Agrostemma githago*	Cornfield	Annual. Pink or white flowers, fertilized by butterflies and moths. Full sun
Cornflower *Centaurea cyanus*	Cornfield	Annual. Available in a range of colours as well as the native blue. Full sun
Cowslip *Primula veris*	Spring meadow	Yellow flower clusters. Prefers limy soil. Sun or partial shade
Daffodil *Narcissuss pseudonarcissus*	Woodland, spring meadow	Spring bulb. Yellow flowers. Sun or partial shade
Field scabious *Knautia arvensis*	Summer meadow	Blue flower heads, popular with moths and bees. Well-drained soil. Full sun
Forget-me-not *Myosotis palustris*	Marsh	Small blue flowers. Damp soil. Full sun or part shade
Germander speedwell *Veronica chamaedrys*	Meadow	Small blue flowers, attractive to bees. Sun or part shade
Harebell *Campanula rotundifolia*	Summer meadow, heath	Violet-blue bellflowers. Native of acid grassland. Well-drained soil. Full sun
Heather *Calluna vulgaris*	Acid heath	Small shrub with rose-purple flowers pollinated by various insects. Acid compost. Full sun
Herb robert *Geranium robertianum*	Wood, meadow, rockland	Lacy leaves and small pink flowers. Sun or partial shade
Knapweed *Centaurea scabiosa*	Summer meadow	Thistle-like flower heads, popular with butterflies. Well-drained soil. Full sun
Marjoram *Origanum vulgare*	Meadow	Aromatic native herb. Poor, well-drained soil. Full sun
Meadow cranesbill *Geranium pratense*	Summer meadow	Perennial. Blue-purple flower heads popular with bees. Full sun
Primrose *Primula vulgaris*	Woodland	Pale yellow flowers. Humus-rich soil. Dappled shade
Red campion *Silene dioica*	Woodland edge	Red flowers. Partial shade
Thrift *Armeria maritima*	Sand dune, shingle	Evergreen tussocks. Pink flower heads. Acid to neutral sandy soil. Full sun
Thyme *Thymus serpyllum*	Heath, meadow, rockland	Small, native evergreen. Mauve flowers popular with bees and butterflies. Limy, well-drained soil. Full sun

*The genus endymion has been renamed hyacinthoides

TABLE 6.2

CONTAINERS

Material	Habitats	Advantages	Disadvantages
Plastic	Woodland, wetland, grassland	Versatile, many shapes and colours, lightweight, cheap, waterproof	May become brittle and crack after a few years
Terracotta/clay	Rockland, woodland, grassland	Attractive. Range of sizes. Good ones long lasting	Porous to water. Large ones expensive. Cheap ones are not frostproof
Ceramic	All	Choice of designs, colours and sizes. Glazed ones are waterproof	Large ones expensive. Cheap ones may not be frostproof
Stone	Rockland, seaside	Attractive texture	Limited colours and shapes. Expensive
Concrete	Rockland, seaside	Cheap but good stone substitute. Can be handmade	Limited range of colours and shapes
Wood	Woodland, shingle, sand dune	Choice of designs, sizes and timber. Can stain or paint. Easily handmade	Cheaper timber needs preservative. Most are not waterproof
Metal	Pool, meadow	Attractive for modern gardens. Can be painted	Heat up quickly in summer. Limited colours and shapes
'Junk', eg old sinks, baths, kitchen containers	All	Usually cheap items from car-boot sales, second hand shops, etc. Interesting and unusual	

Heathland habitat in a clay drainage junction

TABLE 6.3

COMPOSTS FOR CONTAINER HABITATS

Compost	Uses	Advantages	Disadvantages
Soil	Woodland, grassland and rockland (not in hanging containers)	Free or cheap. Heavy, so stable for larger plants	Contains weed seeds. May be too fertile for wildflowers
Soil-based, eg John Innes seed or No. 1	Woodland, grassland and rockland (not in hanging containers)	Heavy, so stable for small trees and shrubs	
Garden compost	Permanent trees and shrubs (not in hanging containers)	Heavy, so stable for larger plants. Free or cheap	Too fertile for most wildflowers. May contain weed seeds and roots
Peat-based	Small woodland, grassland	Good structure, suitable for most plants	Conservation concerns; peat is a non-renewable resource. Difficult to re-wet if dry
Peatless, eg coir-based, composted bark chippings	Small woodland, grassland	Often low fertility, ideal for wildflowers. Recycled waste material	Some may need mixing with grit or perlite to improve drainage
Ericaceous compost	Acid heath plants	Necessary for heathers and other acid lovers	Contains peat, a non-renewable resource. Difficult to re-wet if dry

Mini marshes in
ceramic containers

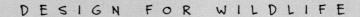

Garden plans

Wildlife gardening is so delightful, there is a good chance you will want to adapt more and more space for wildlife. The end point of this process is the wildlife garden. Of course, how far you go along this path is entirely up to you.

WILDLIFE VERSUS HUMANS

A keen gardener and conservationist I once met told me that his idea of a perfect garden was 'to let the wildflowers grow right up to my doorstep'. Gardens are individual things, reflecting their owners' needs and desires. Remember, though, that in a well-planned garden there is room for humans and wildlife; their requirements need not be in conflict.

You may have a bare, boring or overgrown bit of land to design from scratch. Or you may be generally satisfied with your garden, but want to adapt it to make it more wildlife friendly. Many of the ideas for designing a garden from first principles are also useful for altering an established plot.

DESIGNING FROM SCRATCH

It is exciting and daunting to design a garden, or even part of one. Popular garden makeover programmes, and articles and pictures in glossy magazines, make it look so easy, but they can overwhelm with ideas. How do you begin to choose a style, decide on features and plants and where to put them?

It is fun and surprisingly easy to create an original design. There are no hard and fast rules – be as conservative or imaginative as you want. It is easier if you follow some basic steps:

1   Analyze your garden and determine its characteristics.
2   Decide what you want, and need, according to these.
3   Plan the layout and planting, bearing in mind that you are catering for both wildlife and people.

ANALYZING YOUR GARDEN

Before making any changes, take a good look at your garden. Some things you cannot alter, including its surroundings, soil type, climate, the style of your house and any legal restrictions such as open planning rules and tree preservation orders. The direction a garden faces is also important; a north-facing garden is shadier and cooler than a south-facing one, and may need the patio halfway down the garden instead of by the house.

SMALL GARDEN WITH HABITATS

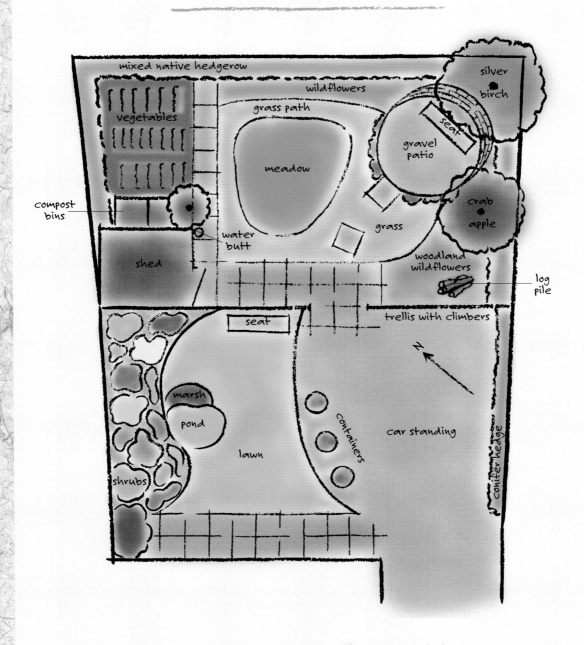

mixed native hedgerow

vegetables

compost bins

wildflowers

grass path

meadow

silver birch

seat

gravel patio

grass

crab apple

water butt

shed

woodland wildflowers

log pile

trellis with climbers

seat

N

marsh

pond

lawn

containers

car standing

shrubs

conifer hedge

The immediate surroundings will also influence your garden design. If you overlook a scenic view, it is unlikely that you will want to hide it; screening may be a priority, on the other hand, if you are overlooked by neighbours or are next to the gasworks.

You are stuck with the style of your house; your garden style should complement it.

Without constant hard work, you are also stuck with your soil type. This affects which plants will grow well in your garden (happy plants in their preferred environment are less likely to succumb to pests and diseases) and may affect your design. If you have a sandy

See Table 7.1
Page 168

KNOW YOUR SOIL

When planning a garden, it is important to know your soil type. This determines what plants grow well, which cultivation methods are suitable, and which habitats will be successful. Peat soil, for example, is acid and retains water, so it is good for marsh and acid heath habitats. Sandy soil, on the other hand, is low in nutrients and free draining, so it is more suitable for meadow and coastal habitats. You can determine what your soil is like with a few simple tests, using equipment that is readily available. The main properties you need to know are how well the soil drains and what its pH value is.

Test for water retention

Clay and peat soils hold water better than sandy and chalk soils. This test shows if your soil is likely to become waterlogged in wet weather, or to dry out quickly in summer.

Fold a piece of kitchen paper into a funnel and place it in a jar for support. Fill a small measuring jug with water and take note of how much it contains. Put a tablespoon

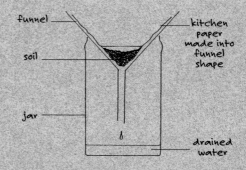

funnel

soil

jar

kitchen paper made into funnel shape

drained water

This simple test shows how well drained your soil is

soil that dries out in summer, it will be difficult for you to cultivate a good lawn; in this case it would be better to have a gravel or hard-standing area of such things as paving, concrete or tar. Table 7.1 suggests habitats suitable for various soil types; of course, you are not limited to these, they are just the ones that would be easiest to establish and manage in your garden.

Climate includes prevailing winds, the effect of which can be reduced by hedges or trees, together with rainfall and temperature extremes, which we have to live with. All of these things should be taken into account when designing or altering a garden.

of dry soil in the funnel, then carefully add water to the centre of the soil, from the jug, making sure none runs down the edge. Stop adding water when the first drop falls into the jar, noting how much you have added, then wait until the soil drains.

Measure the volume of the drained water; if over half of the added water is recovered, your soil is well drained and probably sandy or chalky. If, on the other hand, most of the added water is retained, your soil is clay, silt or peat. Wet clay soil is like Plasticine and silt feels silky, while peat and other soils rich in humus are spongy and can be 'wrung out' when wet.

Test for pH

A simple test, to find if your soil is acidic, alkaline or neutral, can be carried out using coloured vegetable juice as a pH indicator.

Chop some beetroot or red cabbage into small pieces, place them in a container and cover them with boiled water or rainwater (cold tap water contains lime which messes up the test). Leave the vegetable to soak for 10 minutes. Meanwhile, stir a teaspoon of soil into about 10ml (1 dessertspoon) of boiled water and allow it to settle.

Add a few drops of the vegetable juice to the water and observe the colour. If it turns blue, your soil is alkaline; if it goes redder, your soil is acid. No colour change means your soil is approximately neutral.

This test will not give as precise results as proprietary kits or meters, but it does give a rough idea of your soil's pH.

ROUGH PLAN OF GARDEN

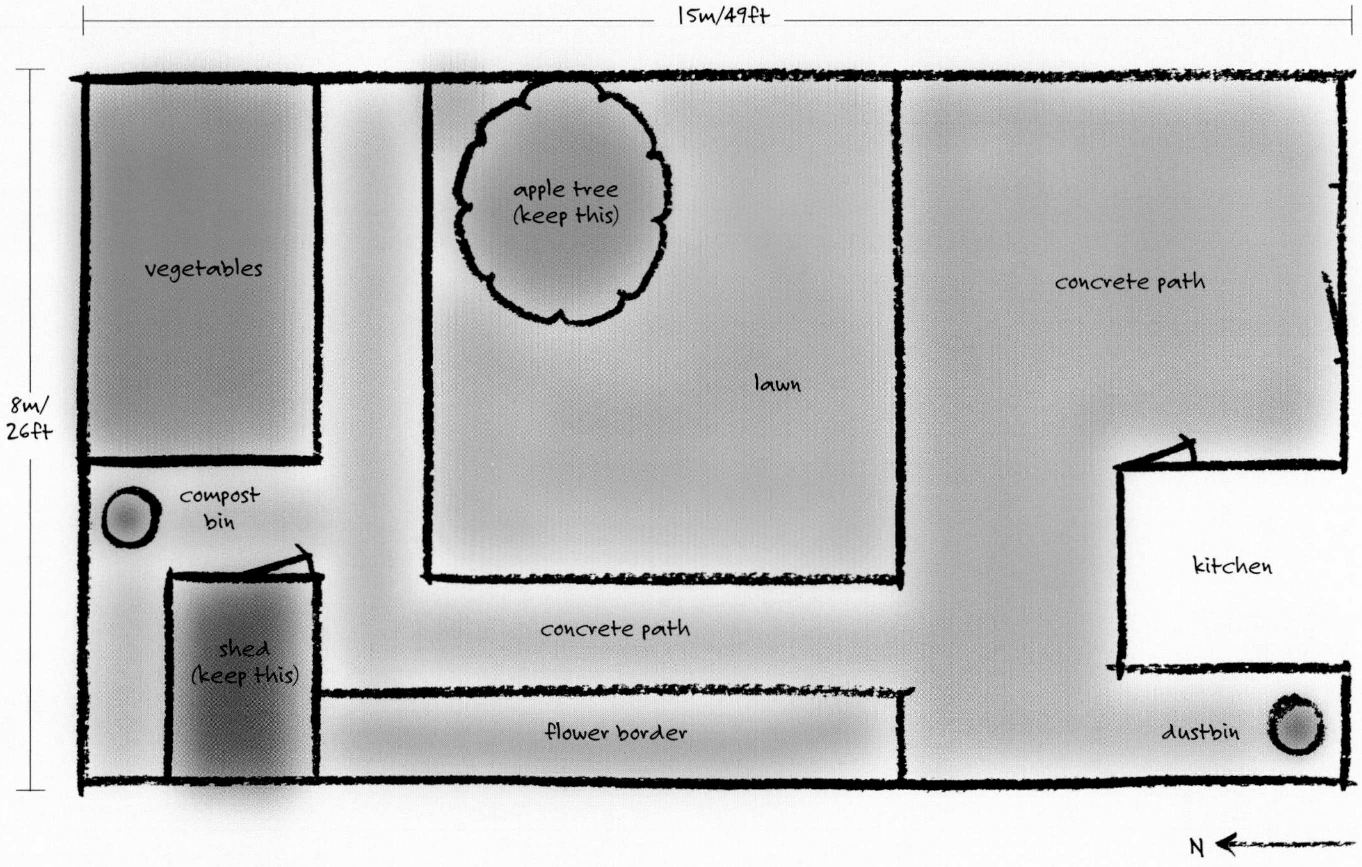

15m/49ft

8m/26ft

concrete path

kitchen

dustbin

N

lawn

apple tree
(keep this)

concrete path

flower border

vegetables

compost
bin

shed
(keep this)

It is useful to draw a rough plan of your garden. This need not be to scale or very detailed at this stage, but approximate measurements are helpful. Include buildings, drives, trees and other major features, and indicate north, any slope, views or eyesores, permanently shady spots, drains and manhole covers, any features you want to keep, and anything else that will be helpful when you redesign the garden. The plan opposite shows the sort of thing required at this stage.

DETERMINING YOUR WANTS AND NEEDS

Deciding what to include in your garden may seem a daunting task. A good way to get organized is to make two lists. The first should consist of essential features, for example a shed, vegetable patch and childrens' play area, as well as necessary evils like the dustbin, washing line and car parking space. The second should note all of the things you and your family would like – a pond, a barbecue, a herb bed . . . This list will almost certainly contain more items than will fit in the space available, and therefore, some compromise will have to be made. It is sensible, especially if space is limited, to prioritize by underlining the things you most want.

It is useful at this stage to think about budget in relation both to construction and upkeep costs. Be realistic, but bear in mind that the whole construction does not have to be done in one go. It can take several years if necessary, as budget and time allow.

Also think about how much time you can and want to spend gardening. A low-maintenance design is better if you are busy, and this is where wildlife gardening can really help because, apart from essential maintenance, habitats do best if they are disturbed as little as possible.

The wants and needs of your family are important. There may be some conflict; for example, your partner may want to grow vegetables for the show bench while you want to attract wildlife, but it should be possible, if sometimes challenging, to cater for everyone.

This is the stage to think about the particular requirements of a wildlife garden. Planting and habitats are more important than style. Although native trees and flowers, meadows, ponds and other habitats look more natural in an informal setting, a formal design can still be wildlife friendly.

PLANNING

Some gardeners prefer not to draw plans, but to 'design' as they go along. There is nothing wrong with this, and excellent results may be obtained. There are good reasons, however, for making a plan.

A plan helps you sort out ideas and allows you to modify them, if necessary, before beginning work. You can decide where to put everything you need and want, and make sure there is sufficient space – can you open the car doors when it is parked in the drive? With a plan mistakes can be put right before they are actually made.

HARD LANDSCAPING

Paths, drives, patios and buildings are the first thing to put into your plan, because these are long-term features and everything else should be fitted around them.

The positions of buildings such as the shed, garage and greenhouse, determine where the paths and drive should go. Try to keep the colour and type of building materials in harmony with those of the house.

Decide what to do with slopes; you might want terraces or a rockery, for instance. Introducing differences in height, with features like raised beds and sunken patios, adds interest to flat sites and provides opportunities for introducing low dry stone walls and rockeries for rockland habitats.

Annual nasturtiums quickly climb a trellis. Their flowers and leaves attract many insects

If you want a water feature, decide where to put it, taking into consideration that electric pumps for waterfalls need buried cables. It is sensible to consult an electrician for any outdoor electrical work.

BOUNDARIES AND SCREENS

There is a good choice of both materials and designs for walls and fences, whether boundary or internal; materials include bricks, stone, concrete blocks, wood and hedges. There is an even wider choice for internal screens. These can be used to separate different parts of the garden, to hide unsightly objects like dustbins and compost heaps, to provide sheltered seating areas, or simply for decoration. Consider dry stone walls, ornamental concrete blocks, woven hurdles, a trellis with climbers, and ornamental flowering hedges, to name just a few. Screens also provide opportunities to introduce rockland habitats, woodland-edge climbers and shrubs which are useful to wildlife.

Fragrant annual sweet peas are useful climbers and attract bees and other flying insects

Your measurements should be accurate to at least the nearest metre (yard). A good method is to draw the outline with a pencil, using an easy scale such as 1cm for every metre, and then draw in the permanent buildings and such things as drives and mature trees that you wish to keep. When you are satisfied with this basic plan, go over it in felt-tip pen.

Next, use a pencil – keeping an eraser to hand – to try out various designs, either directly on the plan or on tracing paper placed over it. A helpful technique is to cut out shapes representing various features, all to the same scale; you can then move these around on the plan, trying out different arrangements, until you are satisfied with their positions. When you are happy, draw them in.

THE HABITATS

A new design or major overhaul of a garden provides an excellent opportunity to incorporate habitats from the start, rather than slotting them in later, and it is better to include several habitats in a wildlife garden.

A new hedge gives you the chance to introduce a woodland-edge habitat, by planting native shrubs. Dry stone walls can become rockland habitats. Trellis screens can be planted with native climbers. Slopes can become rockeries with streams and pools. A shady area can become a wood, planted with shade-loving wildflowers. A boggy area can become a marsh. Nesting boxes can be sited on shady walls amongst ivy. Log piles can be placed in the shrubbery.

Since chemicals are avoided in a wildlife garden, it is impossible to have a weed-free lawn. However good your management,

Thyme forms an attractive ornamental lawn in a small garden

'weeds' will certainly appear. To attract wildlife without inconveniencing the humans too much, leave some of the grass uncut until early summer to create a spring meadow.

A car parking area or drive can double as a habitat; plant some low-growing rockland plants, which do not mind being driven over or walked on occasionally, into the gaps.

PLANTING

Now that you have the basic design, think about what to grow. Bearing in mind that your plot is a garden, not a nature reserve, you need not be restricted to native species, unless you want to be. Tables 7.2–7.4 (see pages 169–71) give examples of garden flowers which are valuable to wildlife, and you are by no means restricted to these. In a wildlife garden there is still room for any plants you fancy, restricted only by space and conditions.

First, decide on long-lived perennials like trees, shrubs, climbers and grass. Few gardens are too small for a tree, which gives height and shade. There is a good choice of native trees and shrubs, some of them very ornamental. (See Tables 2.1 and 2.2, pages 51 and 53, for ideas.) Bear in mind a tree's growth rate, eventual height, spread and shape and seasonal interest. Including at least one evergreen tree or shrub provides winter interest and shelter for roosting and nesting birds.

Filling in between the hard landscaping and permanent plants with annuals, biennials and herbaceous perennials is one of the most enjoyable aspects of gardening. It can be changed every year, so you can try out different plants and colour schemes, and mistakes can be easily rectified.

See Tables 7.2–7.4
Pages 169–71

See Tables 2.1 and 2.2
Pages 51 and 53

A mixed flowerbed attracts beneficial insects into a garden

ORNAMENTAL PLANTS FOR WILDLIFE

Until now I have looked solely at native plants for garden habitats. It is unlikely, however, that you would want to fill the whole garden with wildflowers alone, and there are many 'normal' garden flowers and shrubs that are useful in a wildlife garden.

Some herbivores can only feed from one or a small number of food plants. Many small creatures, on the other hand, are not so fussy. Bees and adult butterflies, for instance, take nectar from almost any flower they can get their mouth parts into, while blackbirds

Garden poppies attract hoverflies and bees

A bumblebee sips nectar from a catmint flower

and thrushes eat winter berries from ornamental and native shrubs.

Some garden plants are more attractive to wildlife than others. Tables 7.2–7.4 (see pages 169–71) suggest useful shrubs and flowers, but there are also many others you might include. To help you choose plants that are likely to attract wildlife, keep the points listed below in mind:

Nicotiana is visited by night moths which are attracted to the flowers by their strong perfume

Buddleia, the butterfly bush, also attracts many other flying insects in late summer, with its fragrant flowers

Open yellow flowers like these marguerites attract hoverflies, whose larvae eat aphids

- Hoverflies seem to prefer yellow or pale blue flowers (although the ones in my garden aren't fussy, going for exotics like fuchsias as well).

- Evergreen shrubs shelter nesting and roosting birds.

- Thorny, informal hedgerows protect nestlings from predators.

- Ground-cover plants of any variety provide shelter for ground beetles, which prey on slugs and vine weevil grubs, helping to keep them in check.

See Tables 7.2–7.4 Pages 169–71

Plants, whether long- or short-term, grow better if they like your soil and conditions, which is why it is worth doing some initial research to determine these beforehand, rather than waste time and money on unsuitable varieties.

ADAPTING AN ESTABLISHED GARDEN

Not everyone wants or is in the position to create a garden from scratch, and most gardeners who have become interested in attracting wildlife are basically happy with their gardens. There are several things you can do to make an existing garden more wildlife friendly; the panel on page 15, The importance of biodiversity, gives some general suggestions.

Take the example of the garden shown in the plan laid out on page 154, which shows the rather boring back garden of a small terraced house. The plan opposite shows the same garden after some simple changes have been made in order to make it more wildlife friendly, and also more attractive for its human occupants.

Familiar in bedding schemes, pansies are descended from the wild viola or heartsease

See Table 7.5 Page 172

This garden has been separated into 'garden rooms' by a row of shrubs and a trellis with climbers. Part of the lawn has been transformed into a spring meadow. Climbers have been planted against boundary walls. A water feature and seating area have been made halfway down the garden to catch the sun. The introduction of native and wildlife-friendly flowers, shrubs and climbers has increased the biodiversity. The garden now has wetland, woodland-edge and grassland habitats.

ADAPTED GARDEN PLAN

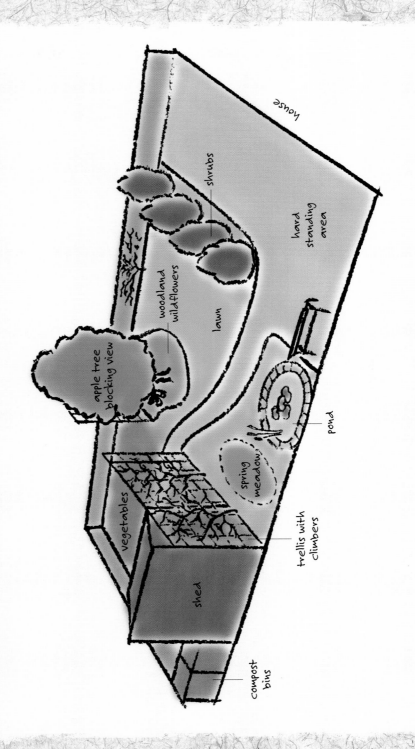

house

shrubs

hard standing area

woodland wildflowers

lawn

apple tree blocking view

pond

spring meadow

trellis with climbers

vegetables

shed

compost bins

VERY SMALL GARDEN OR YARD

Asters provide autumn nectar which is important for over-wintering butterflies

Many modern estate houses – and many old ones too – have tiny back gardens. In my view, a lawn in a very small garden is hardly worth the time, effort and expense of buying a lawn mower. A small, grassless lawn of creeping plants, like white clover, thyme or sedum, attracts insects when the plants are in bloom and looks far nicer than a patch of grass – and it can be walked on occasionally. Hard-standing alternatives include paving, bricks or gravel.

Some older houses have tiny paved yards. We used to live in a back-to-back terrace with such a yard (and in addition, north facing), and managed to grow an imaginative variety of plants in raised beds, edged by low brick walls, filled with a layer of rubble and topped with soil. We supplemented these with shrubs in containers and summer hanging baskets. An alternative for a paved yard would be to remove some slabs, improve the soil with organic matter and fertilizer, and plant small shrubs, herbs and low-growing plants. Water features and container habitats are useful in the smallest gardens.

In a small garden, boundary walls and fences provide important extra room for climbing plants, wall shrubs and hanging containers, so make the most of these. A perennial background of climbers or wall shrubs, such as ivy or pyracantha, can be enhanced in summer with climbing annuals, like nasturtiums and sweet peas, which attract bees and other insects with their colourful blooms.

When choosing plants for a small garden, whether native or ornamental, it is especially important to select plants which are interesting and useful for

Tulips support insects in spring

Useful ornaments like birdbaths make attractive features in a small garden

most of the year. These might include evergreen climbers and shrubs, bushes with flowers followed by colourful berries, and flowers like teasels and honesty which have long-lasting, ornamental seed heads that provide food for seed-eating birds.

Features such as birdbaths, nesting boxes, bird feeders, low, dry stone walls, log piles and rockeries can all be included in a small garden, adding interest and wildlife-friendliness.

FRONT GARDENS

This book has concentrated mainly on back gardens, which are used for recreation and relaxation in relative privacy. Front gardens, on the other hand, are for show; people may be reluctant to use their front gardens for wildlife, because they worry that neighbours may not be sympathetic.

A wildlife-friendly garden need not be a wilderness. I prefer not to have a lawn in my front garden as there are so many more interesting things to do with the space, though I suspect that many gardeners disagree with me and like their green swards. However, setting aside a small patch as a spring meadow does not detract from the lawn and adds interest to the garden. Near where I live, the owner of a very grand front garden has done just that, planting cowslips and spring bulbs, and it looks great.

Growing ornate wildflowers and shrubs is another possibility, as is making a water feature. An evergreen hedge of holly, yew or native privet can be trimmed just as neatly as one consisting of the more usual Japanese privet (*Ligustrum japonicum*) or leylandii (x *Cupressocyparis leylandii*). Ivy or honeysuckle can be trained to grow up the wall of your house.

There may be room for a rockery, if desired. If your front garden is large, consider a small native tree like crab apple or rowan, underplanted with woodland wildflowers.

You can see how small habitats like woodland, wetland, rockland and grassland can easily be included in an ornamental garden. These ideas for a neat, wildlife-friendly front garden can also be transported to the back garden for gardeners who prefer a manicured look.

This wild rose provides food and shelter for wildlife and colourful displays of both flowers and hips

See Table 7.5 Page 172

This example is fairly typical of a small back garden. Many gardens do not fit this mould, however, and have challenges of their own. The panels on pages 164–7 look at particular garden types and how they might be adapted for wildlife; other situations are included in Table 7.5 (see page 172), with suggestions for solving the challenges each presents.

BALCONY OR ROOF GARDEN

Containers are the obvious thing for these situations (see Chapter 6 for ideas). Before siting anything except small containers, make sure you know the weight-bearing capacity of your roof or balcony. This may mean getting a survey done, but this is cheaper than repairs if something collapses.

Balconies and roof gardens are usually exposed to the elements. In these respects they are similar to natural cliffs and hillsides, and upland heaths and grasslands. This gives an idea of the types of plants that will grow well, and the habitats you might use. Because of their exposure, containers at height need regular watering even more than those at ground level and for this, a built-in irrigation system saves time.

On a roof garden or large balcony, you may be able to rig up some shelter in the form of a fence or trellis with hardy climbers like ivy. Raised beds and even water features could be built round the edges, above supporting walls. Shrubs which grow successfully in such conditions include wild and garden roses, honeysuckle, lilac, broom and buddleia.

High-rise gardens can provide safe sanctuaries for feeding and nesting birds, away from cats and squirrels.

THE FUTURE OF WILDLIFE GARDENING

The increasing popularity of wildlife gardening reflects growing concerns about rural habitat loss. As more of us design or modify our gardens to encourage wildlife, it may encourage others to follow suit. Maybe one day most public parks and gardens will contain areas of open woodland and meadows. As I put the finishing touches to this book, in the first month of the third millennium, it is encouraging to know that a flagship organic garden and conservation area has recently been created around the Dome at Greenwich, in London, to attract creatures present decades ago back to the site. If this is a sign of things to come, we can look forward with optimism, but I hope I have shown that we can all play a part, however small, in supporting wildlife.

TABLE 7.1

SOIL TYPES AND HABITATS

Soil	Properties	Water retention	pH	Suggested habitats
Clay	Very small particles. Hard lumps when dry, sticky when wet. Heavy	Very good	Any	Marsh, grassland, woodland
Silt	Small particles. Smooth to the touch	Good	Any	Grassland, marsh, woodland
Sand	Gritty, with large particles. Easy to dig	Poor	Any	Grassland, coast, woodland
Chalk	Crumbly, with flints. Pale and shallow	Poor	Alkaline	Chalk grassland, coast, rockland
Peat	Soft and spongy. Dark brown or black	Very good	Acid	Acid heath, marsh

TABLE 7.2

ORNAMENTAL SHRUBS OF VALUE TO WILDLIFE

Shrub	Value to wildlife
Barberry *Berberis thunbergii*	Birds eat scarlet berries in autumn and winter. Spiky leaves give protection to nesting birds in spring
Buddleia *Buddleia davidii*	Nectar for butterflies, including peacocks, small tortoiseshells, red admirals, commas and brimstones
Cotoneaster *Cotoneaster* spp.	Red winter berries for blackbirds, waxwings and other birds. Bush varieties make secure nesting sites
Firethorn *Pyracantha* spp.	Frothy white flowers attract insects. Blackbirds eat the berries in early winter; red fruits are eaten before orange ones
Flowering currant *Ribes sanguineum*	Rose-red flowers provide spring nectar for bees.
Hebe *Hebe* spp.	Spires of mauve, pink or white flowers attract peacock, red admiral, small tortoiseshell and other butterflies
Japanese quince *Chaenomeles speciosa*	Red, pink or white spring flowers attract bees and butterflies. Blackbirds and thrushes eat fallen autumn fruit
Lavender *Lavandula* spp.	Nectar for butterflies and bees. Birds eat seeds
Mahonia *Mahonia* spp.	Scented yellow flowers provide early spring nectar. Birds eat the berries of *M. aquifolium*
Rosemary *Rosmarinus officinalis*	Pale lilac flowers attract bees, butterflies and hoverflies
Thyme *Thymus* spp.	Lilac or pink flowers attract bees and butterflies
Viburnum *Viburnum* spp.	Scented winter flowers provide nectar for early insects

Barberry

Flowering currant

TABLE 7.3

ORNAMENTAL ANNUALS AND BIENNIALS OF VALUE TO WILDLIFE

Plant	Flowers	Value to wildlife
Californian poppy *Eschscholzia californica*	Orange-yellow; June–September	Flowers attract hoverflies
Candytuft *Iberis umbellata*	Pink, mauve or white clusters; June–September	Nectar for butterflies
Clarkia *Clarkia elegans*	White, mauve, orange or scarlet; July–September	Flowers attract bees
Evening primrose *Oenothera biennis*	Pale yellow; June–August	Flowers provide nectar for night moths. Hoverflies visit flowers during morning
French marigold *Tagetes patula*	Orange-brown and yellow; June–autumn	Nectar for butterflies
Honesty *Lunaria biennis*	Mauve or white; April–June	Nectar for butterflies. Food plant for the caterpillars of orange-tip butterflies. Bullfinches eat seeds from white, disc-shaped seed pods
Larkspur *Delphinium consolida* syn. *Consolida ambigua, C. ajacis*	Blue, purple, red, pink or white; June–August	Flowers attract bees
Nasturtium *Tropaeolum majus*	Yellow, orange or red; June–September	Flowers attract bees and hoverflies
Poached-egg flower *Limnanthes douglasii*	Yellow and white; June–August	Flowers attract hoverflies and bees
Pot marigold *Calendula officinalis*	Orange or yellow; May–autumn	Flowers attract hoverflies and wasps
Snapdragon *Antirrhinum majus*	Various colours; July–autumn	Flowers attract bumblebees
Sunflower *Helianthus annus*	Large yellow daisy-like flowers; July–September	Flowers attract bees and butterflies. Goldfinches and other birds eat the seeds
Sweet rocket *Hesperis matronalis*	Mauve or white; June	Flowers attract butterflies and moths
Tobacco plant *Nicotiana alata*	White, pink, crimson or yellow; June–September	Nectar attracts hawk moths and other night moths
Virginian stock *Malcolmia maritima*	Red, lilac, pink or white; summer	Flowers attract bees
Wallflower *Cheiranthus cheiri**	White, yellow, orange or red; April–June	Flowers attract insects

*The genus cheiranthus has been renamed erysimum

French marigold

TABLE 7.4

PERENNIALS OF VALUE TO WILDLIFE

Plant	Flowers	Value to wildlife
Achillea *Achillea filipendulina*	Yellow clusters; summer	Flowers attract hoverflies. Seeds eaten by sparrows, greenfinches and tits
Chives *Allium schoenoprasum*	Rose-pink flower heads; June–July	Flowers attract bees and butterflies
Comfrey *Symphytum* x *uplandicum*	Blue or purple; June–August	Moth and butterfly caterpillars eat the leaves
Cranesbill *Geranium* spp.	Pink or mauve; summer	Flowers attract bees. Seeds eaten by bullfinches
Fennel *Foeniculum vulgare*	Gold-yellow umbels; July–August	Flowers attract hoverflies, bees and wasps. Leaves eaten by caterpillars
Globe thistle *Echinops ritro*	Globular blue flower heads; July–August	Nectar for bees. Seeds eaten by gold- and greenfinches
Golden rod *Solidago canadensis*	Yellow clusters; August–October	Nectar for butterflies, moths and other insects. Seeds eaten by birds
Ice-plant *Sedum spectabile*	Pink or mauve clusters; September–October	Nectar for butterflies and bumblebees
Michaelmas daisy *Aster novi-belgii*	Mauve, crimson or pink; September–October	Nectar for small tortoiseshell and other butterflies
Mullein *Verbascum* spp.	Yellow or pink spires; summer	Mullein moth caterpillar eats leaves
Oriental poppy *Papaver orientale*	Scarlet, pink, orange or white; May–June	Flowers attract bees
Phlox *Phlox paniculata*	White, pink, red, or purple; July–September	Nectar for butterflies and moths
Yellow alyssum *Alyssum saxatile*	Bright yellow; April–June	Nectar for orange-tip, small tortoiseshell, peacock and other butterflies
Winter aconite *Eranthis hyemalis*	Lemon yellow; early spring	Pollen for bees, flies and other insects

Mullein

Cranesbill

TABLE 7.5

SOLUTIONS TO SPECIAL AND CHALLENGING SITUATIONS
(continued next page)

Situation	Problems	Solutions
Front garden	Ornamental, so generally kept tidy	Wildlife-friendly ornamental plants. Small spring meadow in lawn. Small water feature
Very small garden or yard	Limited space	Use boundary walls and fences for climbing plants. Replace lawn with paving, scree or low-growing ornamentals. Raised beds and containers. Native or ornamental plants with seasonal interest
Shady	Limited planting. Soil may be dry	Woodland plants and other shade lovers. Variegated shrubs and climbers (eg holly, ivy). Add organic matter and mulch and water if dry
Boggy	Limited planting. Difficult to cultivate	Drain if serious problem. Grow marshland wildflowers and suitable ornamentals. Plant alder, willow or dogwood, coppicing or pruning if required
Steep slope	Difficult to cultivate. Dry at top and possible frost pocket at bottom	Create tiers, with brick or dry stone walls. Rockland, possibly with pool and stream. Plant ground cover (eg ivy, periwinkle, and prostrate conifer)
Hot and dry	Limited planting. Little or no shade	Incorporate organic matter and mulch. Plant rockland and seaside plants. Scree bed or rockery habitat
Near coast	Salty winds. Often dry, sandy or chalk soil. Limited planting	Incorporate organic matter and mulch. Plant seaside natives and tolerant ornamentals. Sand dune or shingle habitat

TABLE 7.5

SOLUTIONS TO SPECIAL AND CHALLENGING SITUATIONS
(continued)

Situation	Problems	Solutions
Windswept	Limited planting. Little or no shelter	Create shelter with hedging or tolerant trees (eg poplar)
Overlooked or ugly view	Need for privacy or shelter	Fences, trellis with climbers or hedges, boundary or internal. Arbours and enclosed areas, with climbers, for privacy
Roof garden	Limited weight bearing. No indigenous soil. Windswept	Have survey to check load-bearing capacity. Containers of suitable plants and habitats. Trellis, with climbers, for shelter. Raised beds and water features
Balcony	Limited space and weight-bearing capacity. Windswept. No indigenous soil	Containers of suitable plants and habitats. Wall containers and hanging baskets
No garden	Limited to wall containers and window boxes	Containers of suitable plants and habitats
Young children	Dangerous plants and features	Avoid plants with poisonous berries (eg yew), thorns or prickly leaves, and caustic sap (eg euphorbias). Avoid open water; bubble fountains and similar features are safe

Glossary

annual – a plant which flowers, produces seeds, then dies, within one year

Bentonite – a proprietary clay pond-lining material, available as a membrane, in blocks, or as powder

Wood anemone

biennial – a plant which flowers and produces seeds in its second year after germination

biodegradable – a substance that will decay naturally, by the action of fungus or microbes, is biodegradable. Most biodegradable materials are naturally-occurring or produced from natural products, eg shredded prunings, paper, old cotton clothes

biodiversity – this refers to the number of different species occupying a given area or habitat; those with a larger biodiversity are healthier and more stable

bonsai – the Japanese art of growing trees in containers, using skilful pruning to keep them small and to form attractive shapes

carnivore – a creature that eats other animals

community – all the living things that occupy a habitat

compost – 1. a growing medium for container plants – 2. material resulting from rapid decomposition of dead plant material, which is a good soil conditioner and mulch

coppice – to cut back a tree or shrub, annually or every few years, for a sustainable timber crop. New growth sprouts from the trunk. Coppicing can also be done in the garden to prevent shrubs from growing too large, or to encourage the growth of attractive young foliage

decomposition – the processing of dead plants and animals, and animal excreta, by fungi and micro-organisms, returning their substances to the environment

detritus – decaying plant matter and animal bodies on pond bottoms

drift – a long, narrow planting of varieties of the same type, weaving among other plants to give a pleasing effect

Hazel catkins

Coppiced willow

ecology – the study of how living things interact with each other and with their environment

ecosystem – a habitat and the living things found there

environment – the non-living world and its properties, eg rocks, atmosphere, climate

food chain – a chain of feeding relationships within or between habitats. Most food chains consist of plants, herbivores, small carnivores and larger carnivores

food web – similar to a food chain, but more complex, and far more common in nature. This describes the links between feeding relationships in or between habitats

group – to plant three or more plants of the same type close together to give a pleasing and natural effect

habitat – the place where an organism lives, eg a wood or pond

harden off – the process of gradually acclimatizing a plant to the outside conditions; if a plant is moved suddenly from indoors to outside, the shock may kill it

hardwood cutting – a cutting of a tree or shrub, taken from ripe wood in autumn

herbaceous plant – a perennial whose foliage dies back every winter, producing new top growth the following year

herbivore – a creature that feeds on vegetation alone

inflorescence – a flower cluster. Many so-called 'flowers' are actually inflorescences, consisting of many small flowers, eg daisy, lupin, yarrow

leaf litter - dead leaves under trees; a rich wildlife habitat

leaf mould – organic material formed from decomposed leaves: a good soil conditioner

loam – good garden soil, with a balance of components

mead – an old word for a flowery meadow

mulch – a layer of material – compost, leaf mould, shredded bark – spread over the soil surface to reduce evaporation of water from the soil and suppress weeds

Herb robert

naturalized plant – a plant species introduced from another country as a garden plant which has subsequently spread into the countryside

organic gardening – gardening in co-operation with nature, using no synthetic chemicals

Purple loosestrife

organic matter – bulky material derived from living or once-living things, eg garden compost, rotted manure, leaf mould, used as soil conditioner and mulch

panicle – a loosely branched inflorescence, as found on whitebeam

perennial – a plant that lives for several years

pH – a measure of acidity or alkalinity. Soils can be acid (pH less than 7), neutral (pH 7) or alkaline (pH greater than 7)

predator – a creature that preys on other creatures. Useful for controlling 'pest' levels

rosette plant – a plant which has a circle of leaves growing from the same point on the ground, eg dandelions, plantains

rotifer – a type of microscopic pond animal, with rings of beating hairs that appear to rotate as it swims

scavenger – a creature that feeds on dead plants or animals

scrambling plant – a plant with spreading stems, which may form mats or intermingle with grass and other plants, eg daisy, clover and speedwell

scree – fallen rock fragments at the foot of a cliff or rock face

semi-ripe cutting – a cutting of a tree or shrub, taken from young growth in early summer

shingle – rounded gravel fragments found on the seashore and river banks

slow-release fertilizer – an organic fertilizer derived from once-living things, eg blood-fish-and-bonemeal, seaweed extract, which releases its nutrients slowly into the soil

springtail – a primitive, wingless invertebrate which can leap by suddenly 'flexing' its body. Springtails are common in leaf litter

stratification – the activation of certain seeds before germination by exposing them to a period of cold. Many seeds of trees, shrubs and wildflowers require stratification before they will germinate

Oxeye daisy

umbel – type of inflorescence with a flat or umbrella-like shape, eg yarrow, cow parsley, fennel

understory shrubs – young trees and wildflowers growing under woodland trees

wildlife corridor – a long, narrow habitat, eg hedge, canal, river, valuable for the migration and spreading of species

Further reading

Baines C., *Wildlife Garden Notebook* (Oxford Illustrated Press, 1984)

— *How to Make a Wildlife Garden* (Elm Tree Books, 1985)

— *The Wild Side of Town* (BBC Publications and Elm Tree Books, 1986)

Bennett J., *The Wildlife Garden Month-by-Month* (David and Charles, 1993)

Bishop O. N., *Natural Communities* (John Murray, 1973)

Hamilton G, *Successful Organic Gardening* (Dorling Kindersley, 1987)

Mabey R. and Evans T., *The Flowering of Britain* (Chatto and Windus, 1989)

Reader's Digest, *Wildlife on Your Doorstep* (Reader's Digest Association Ltd, 1986)

Sykes L., *The Natural Hedgehog* (Gaia Books Ltd, 1995)

Organic Gardening magazine (Organic Gardening)

Useful addresses

CANADA

Canadian Wildlife Federation
350 Michael Cowpland Drive, Kanata,
Ontario K2M 2W1

Canadian Wildlife Service
Environment Canada, Ottawa,
Ontario K1A 0H3

The Garden Institute
Box 1406, Calgary Trail, Edmonton,
Alberta T6J 5M8

Terra Viva Organics
505-1009 Expo Boulevard, Vancouver,
British Columbia V6Z 2V9

UNITED KINGDOM

The Countryside Agency
John Dower House, Crescent Place,
Cheltenham, Gloucestershire GL50 3RA

English Nature
Northminster House, Peterborough PR1 1UA

HDRA: The Organic Organisation
(formerly Henry Doubleday Reasearch
Association)
Ryton-on-Dunsmore, Coventry CV8 3LG

Landlife
(formerly Rural Preservation Association)
The National Wildflower Centre,
Court Hey Park, Liverpool L16 3NA

**Natural Surroundings Centre for Wildlife
Gardening and Conservation**
Bayfield Estate, Holt, Norfolk NR25 7JN

The National Trust
PO Box 39, Bromley, Kent BR1 3XL

**The Royal Society for the Protection of
Birds** (RSPB)
The Lodge, Sandy, Bedfordshire SG19 2DL

Woodland Trust
Autumn Park, Dysart Road, Grantham
Lincolnshire NG31 6LL

UNITED STATES

Defenders of Wildlife
National Headquarters, 1101 14th Street,
NW #1400, Washington DC 20005

Oklahoma Organic Gardening Association
PO Box 74974, Oklahoma City,
Oklahoma 73147

U.S. Fish and Wildlife Service
Division of Habitat Conservation,
1849 C Street NW, Room 400,
Arlington Square, Washington DC 20240

The Wildlife Society
5410 Grosvenor Lane, Bethesda,
Maryland 20814

About the author

Josie Briggs is a keen organic gardener, with an emphasis on wildlife gardening. She has written articles for several publications, including *Organic Gardening*, *Suffolk and Norfolk Life*, *Country Gardens*, *Amateur Gardening*, *Aquarist and Pondkeeper* and *The Countryman*. She has also written a book about wildlife conservation in Norfolk, *Walks in the Wilds of Norfolk*.

Josie is a tutor in chemistry and biology. She lives with her husband in Norfolk.

Index

TITLES AVAILABLE FROM
GMC Publications

BOOKS

Woodcarving

The Art of the Woodcarver	*GMC Publications*
Carving Architectural Detail in Wood:	
The Classical Tradition	*Frederick Wilbur*
Carving Birds & Beasts	*GMC Publications*
Carving Nature: Wildlife Studies in Wood	*Frank Fox-Wilson*
Carving Realistic Birds	*David Tippey*
Decorative Woodcarving	*Jeremy Williams*
Elements of Woodcarving	*Chris Pye*
Essential Tips for Woodcarvers	*GMC Publications*
Essential Woodcarving Techniques	*Dick Onians*
Further Useful Tips for Woodcarvers	*GMC Publications*
Lettercarving in Wood: A Practical Course	*Chris Pye*
Making & Using Working Drawings for	
Realistic Model Animals	*Basil F. Fordham*
Power Tools for Woodcarving	*David Tippey*
Practical Tips for Turners & Carvers	*GMC Publications*
Relief Carving in Wood: A Practical Introduction	*Chris Pye*
Understanding Woodcarving	*GMC Publications*
Understanding Woodcarving in the Round	*GMC Publications*
Useful Techniques for Woodcarvers	*GMC Publications*
Wildfowl Carving – Volume 1	*Jim Pearce*
Wildfowl Carving – Volume 2	*Jim Pearce*
Woodcarving: A Complete Course	*Ron Butterfield*
Woodcarving: A Foundation Course	*Zoë Gertner*
Woodcarving for Beginners	*GMC Publications*
Woodcarving Tools & Equipment	
Test Reports	*GMC Publications*
Woodcarving Tools, Materials & Equipment	*Chris Pye*

Woodturning

Adventures in Woodturning	*David Springett*
Bert Marsh: Woodturner	*Bert Marsh*
Bowl Turning Techniques Masterclass	*Tony Boase*
Colouring Techniques for Woodturners	*Jan Sanders*
Contemporary Turned Wood: New Perspectives	
in a Rich Tradition	*Ray Leier, Jan Peters & Kevin Wallace*
The Craftsman Woodturner	*Peter Child*
Decorative Techniques for Woodturners	*Hilary Bowen*
Fun at the Lathe	*R.C. Bell*
Further Useful Tips for Woodturners	*GMC Publications*
Illustrated Woodturning Techniques	*John Hunnex*
Intermediate Woodturning Projects	*GMC Publications*
Keith Rowley's Woodturning Projects	*Keith Rowley*
Practical Tips for Turners & Carvers	*GMC Publications*
Turning Green Wood	*Michael O'Donnell*
Turning Miniatures in Wood	*John Sainsbury*
Turning Pens and Pencils	*Kip Christensen & Rex Burningham*
Understanding Woodturning	*Ann & Bob Phillips*
Useful Techniques for Woodturners	*GMC Publications*
Useful Woodturning Projects	*GMC Publications*
Woodturning: Bowls, Platters, Hollow Forms, Vases,	
Vessels, Bottles, Flasks, Tankards, Plates	*GMC Publications*
Woodturning: A Foundation Course	
(New Edition)	*Keith Rowley*

Woodturning: A Fresh Approach	*Robert Chapman*
Woodturning: An Individual Approach	*Dave Regester*
Woodturning: A Source Book of Shapes	*John Hunnex*
Woodturning Jewellery	*Hilary Bowen*
Woodturning Masterclass	*Tony Boase*
Woodturning Techniques	*GMC Publications*
Woodturning Tools & Equipment	
Test Reports	*GMC Publications*
Woodturning Wizardry	*David Springett*

Woodworking

Bird Boxes and Feeders for the Garden	*Dave Mackenzie*
Complete Woodfinishing	*Ian Hosker*
David Charlesworth's Furniture-Making	
Techniques	*David Charlesworth*
Furniture & Cabinetmaking Projects	*GMC Publications*
Furniture-Making Projects for the	
Wood Craftsman	*GMC Publications*
Furniture-Making Techniques for	
the Wood Craftsman	*GMC Publications*
Furniture Projects	*Rod Wales*
Furniture Restoration (Practical Crafts)	*Kevin Jan Bonner*
Furniture Restoration and Repair	
for Beginners	*Kevin Jan Bonner*
Furniture Restoration Workshop	*Kevin Jan Bonner*
Green Woodwork	*Mike Abbott*
Kevin Ley's Furniture Projects	*Kevin Ley*
Making & Modifying Woodworking Tools	*Jim Kingshott*
Making Chairs and Tables	*GMC Publications*
Making Classic English Furniture	*Paul Richardson*
Making Little Boxes from Wood	*John Bennett*
Making Shaker Furniture	*Barry Jackson*
Making Woodwork Aids and Devices	*Robert Wearing*
Minidrill: Fifteen Projects	*John Everett*
Pine Furniture Projects for the Home	*Dave Mackenzie*
Practical Scrollsaw Patterns	*John Everett*
Router Magic: Jigs, Fixtures and Tricks to	
Unleash your Router's Full Potential	*Bill Hylton*
Routing for Beginners	*Anthony Bailey*
The Scrollsaw: Twenty Projects	*John Everett*
Sharpening: The Complete Guide	*Jim Kingshott*
Sharpening Pocket Reference Book	*Jim Kingshott*
Simple Scrollsaw Projects	*GMC Publications*
Space-Saving Furniture Projects	*Dave Mackenzie*
Stickmaking: A Complete Course	*Andrew Jones & Clive George*
Stickmaking Handbook	*Andrew Jones & Clive George*
Test Reports: *The Router* and *Furniture*	
& Cabinetmaking	*GMC Publications*
Veneering: A Complete Course	*Ian Hosker*
Woodfinishing Handbook (Practical Crafts)	*Ian Hosker*
Woodworking with the Router:	
Professional Router Techniques	
any Woodworker can Use	*Bill Hylton & Fred Matlack*
The Workshop	*Jim Kingshott*

Upholstery

Toymaking

Dolls' Houses and Miniatures

Crafts

Gardening

VIDEOS

Drop-in and Pinstuffed Seats	*David James*	Twists and Advanced Turning	*Dennis White*
Stuffover Upholstery	*David James*	Sharpening the Professional Way	*Jim Kingshott*
Elliptical Turning	*David Springett*	Sharpening Turning & Carving Tools	*Jim Kingshott*
Woodturning Wizardry	*David Springett*	Bowl Turning	*John Jordan*
Turning Between Centres: The Basics	*Dennis White*	Hollow Turning	*John Jordan*
Turning Bowls	*Dennis White*	Woodturning: A Foundation Course	*Keith Rowley*
Boxes, Goblets and Screw Threads	*Dennis White*	Carving a Figure: The Female Form	*Ray Gonzalez*
Novelties and Projects	*Dennis White*	The Router: A Beginner's Guide	*Alan Goodsell*
Classic Profiles	*Dennis White*	The Scroll Saw: A Beginner's Guide	*John Burke*

MAGAZINES

WOODTURNING
WOODCARVING
FURNITURE & CABINETMAKING
THE ROUTER
WOODWORKING
THE DOLLS' HOUSE MAGAZINE
WATER GARDENING
EXOTIC GARDENING
GARDEN CALENDAR
OUTDOOR PHOTOGRAPHY
BUSINESSMATTERS

The above represents a full list of all titles currently published or scheduled to be published.
All are available direct from the Publishers or through bookshops, newsagents and specialist retailers.
To place an order, or to obtain a complete catalogue, contact:

GMC PUBLICATIONS

Castle Place, 166 High Street, Lewes, East Sussex BN7 1XU, United Kingdom
Tel: 01273 488005 Fax: 01273 478606
E-mail: pubs@thegmcgroup.com

Orders by credit card are accepted